AF538283

A Time for YOUTH

Hoyt W. Brewster, Jr.

Bookcraft
Salt Lake City, Utah

Quoted material herein taken from the *Ensign* and the *New Era* is used by permission of The Church of Jesus Christ of Latter-day Saints

Library of Congress Catalog Card Number: 89-60625

ISBN 0-88494-698-3

First Printing, 1989

Printed in the United States of America

To youth, young adults,
and leaders of youth:

"O youth of the noble birthright,
Carry on, carry on, carry on!"

(Hymns, 255)

Contents

Preface

Youth is a glorious time of life. There are so many things for you to learn. Change often seems to be the only constant. Your bodies and your minds continue to stretch as they seek full development. You feel new sensations. Divinely placed longings begin to awaken from a deep and sacred slumber. Life is wonderful. Yet you may also feel those often nearly overwhelming frustrations that are so much a part of youthful experience.

Youth is filled with challenges, not the least of which is a desire to be independent while still having to depend upon Mom and Dad or other loved ones for some very basic needs of life. Many answers which have been accepted since childhood come under question as you struggle to establish a value system and a way of thinking to which you can be really committed. Sometimes you may make mistakes as you test unknown waters or even try toe-dipping and surfing in areas which are clearly marked "Danger!"

Youth is a time of life often worshipped by society. Major advertising campaigns promote the promise of a return to looking and feeling youthful by using certain products. Growing old is often portrayed very disparagingly. "Never before has there been so much emphasis on youth and beauty," noted Elder Paul H. Dunn. "While youth and beauty are cherished attributes, age and experience can be tremendous assets." (*Ensign*, Nov. 1983, p. 26.)

In your quest to experience life to its fullest, be careful that you don't turn aside the wisdom of those who are no longer young in years but still remain young in spirit. Someone wisely said, "Youth is not a time of life; it is a state of mind. . . . Nobody grows old merely by living a number of years. We grow old by deserting our ideals.''

Why do I title this book *A Time for Youth?* Not because of the stress placed upon youth by mass marketing campaigns, but because you young people will play a significant role in the unfolding drama of events during some very critical times in our world's history.

In order for you to accomplish your purposes in life, it is important that you know who you really are, what your potential is, and how you can develop the skills to reach that potential.

This book has been divided into three parts. Part one focuses on the theme of *myself*, addressing such questions as ''Who am I?'' ''What is my potential?'' ''How do my decisions determine whether I reach that potential?'' and ''What things are most important to me?'' Part two discusses how you can improve your relationships with others, offering helpful suggestions on such issues as ''How can I make friends?'' ''How can I resist pressure to join in the wrong kinds of activities?'' ''How can I improve my ability to communicate with others?'' ''What do I need to know about dating?'' and ''How can I be a leader?'' Part three is the capstone of everything and focuses on our coming unto Christ. If we can truly learn how to do this, everything else will ultimately fall into its proper place in our lives.

Speaking to the youth of the Church, President Ezra Taft Benson said: ''You have been born at this time for a sacred and glorious purpose. It is not by chance that you have been reserved to come to earth in this last dispensation of the fulness of times. Your birth at this particular time was foreordained in the eternities.'' (*Ensign*, May 1986, p. 43; also *Ensign*, Nov. 1986, p. 81.)

Think of it! Of all the billions of people who have inhabited this earth (some estimate this number at fifty or sixty billion), you were selected to come to earth at this most significant period of earth's history. You are here to accomplish some great good.

A prophet of God has said, "We are rearing a royal generation . . . who have special things to do" (Spencer W. Kimball, *Ensign*, May 1976, p. 45).

While the world may focus on youth for the wrong reasons, the people of this planet will yet be lifted, edified, and saved by the "youth of the noble birthright" who carry a conviction of Christ in their hearts.

Bishop Glenn L. Pace has offered the following wise counsel to youth:

> I know how much you like thrills, adventure, and excitement. Do you want excitement? I'll give you excitement. Do you realize you are outnumbered in the world 1,000 to 1? The sons of Helaman didn't face those odds. As the winds of popular opinion intensify and the mocking increases from those who are trying to justify their own unrighteous actions, you will be required to put on the full armor of God. You will need to fight with all of your strength to keep unspotted from the world. We plead with you to stay true—not for us, but for you.
>
> With odds of 1,000 to 1, shall the youth of Zion falter? I give a firm testimony. No! Never! The youth of the kingdom will emerge victorious. Now that's exciting! What adventure in that great and spacious building would you trade for the thrill and excitement of building the very kingdom the Savior will come to the earth to govern?
>
> We love you, the youth of the Church, and we know you will collectively succeed. However, we have great anxiety for individuals we may lose along

> the way. Speaking as a father, I can tell you the loss of one of you is too many. We want each and every one of you to succeed, not just the majority. (*Ensign*, Nov. 1987, pp. 40–41.)

Today is truly a time for youth!

Knowing and Improving Myself

I

1

Your Divine Potential

"*Be all that you can be!*" This phrase from a clever advertising campaign could well serve as a rallying call for you to live up to your divine potential. To become all that you were intended to be is to live up to the measure of your creation (see D&C 88:19).

Have you ever contemplated your real potential?

Some seem satisfied with being less than their best. Sometimes this is because they don't recognize their true potential. Their story becomes similar to that of the mixed-up eagle.

An orphaned eaglet was discovered by a farmer who took the young bird to his farm and raised it among his chickens. As the bird grew, it failed to recognize its magnificent potential to soar among the clouds. It was content to scratch in the dirt with the chickens.

One day a naturalist drove by the farm and saw the eagle among the chickens. He stopped and asked the farmer why the bird was confined to the chicken coop. "Because he's a chicken," replied the farmer. The naturalist asked for and was given permission to try to teach the eagle its true identity. He took the bird to the top of the barn and said to it, "You are an eagle! Fly!" Then he gently threw the bird into the air, but it simply fluttered to the ground where it resumed its association with the chickens, scratching in the dirt.

"I told you that bird was no eagle," observed the farmer.

Discouraged but undaunted, the naturalist asked permission to try one more time to teach the eagle its true nature. The farmer agreed, and before dawn the next morning the naturalist took the eagle to a nearby mountain peak. Climbing the eastern slope, the man and bird reached the top shortly before sunrise. Just as the sun's rays began to rise above the surface of the distant earth, the naturalist held the eagle over the edge of a protruding ridge and said: "You are an eagle! You are to fly among the clouds!" With that he firmly yet kindly threw the eagle into the open space beyond the ridge. At first the bird began to fall, but then its true nature took hold. It spread its wings and, catching a current of wind, soared into the sky. The eagle had discovered its true identity. It now began to fulfill its divinely decreed potential.

What about you? Have you discovered and accepted your true identity?

The story of the eagle and the chickens reminds me of another bird story—*Jonathan Livingston Seagull.* Jonathan was a bird who was not content to be just another seagull, spending all his time searching for food. For him the thing that mattered most was flying. While the other seagulls spent their time and energy satisfying their insatiable appetite for food, Jonathan soared in the skies, practicing new flying techniques. He wanted to become all that he could be, to exceed the self-imposed limits on flying skills that the other birds so willingly accepted.

As you view your role in life, consider how you can most profitably use your time and talents. Are you content to be numbered among the masses of people who mundanely pursue a course designed to satisfy their material or physical appetites and who seemingly have no interest in developing skills of a higher order?

In a way, you have been sent to earth by a loving Father in Heaven to learn how to fly. An Apostle and counselor in the First Presidency of the Church, President Hugh B. Brown, made the following observation: "Each man is the pilot of his own life, charged with the responsibility of the flight across the valley of life and over the hills of eternity. Keep this in mind as you ponder the thought that the creator is your Father —heed His warnings, for His purpose is to help you make a happy landing." (*Church News*, Nov. 13, 1965, p. C-2.)

You are here to receive "pilot's" training; in a sense, you are here on earth to *earn your wings.* A critical factor in the safety of any pilot is his ability to listen to authorized instructions and strictly follow them. The slightest deviation can prove fatal.

Man's third landing on the moon was to have taken place in 1970 with the launching of Apollo 13. The launch and first 205,000 miles of flawless flight brought smiles of satisfaction to all connected with the project. However, on the third day of flight a problem was discovered. One of two essential oxygen tanks aboard the service module had exploded and the other was leaking. Of course, the landing on the moon was aborted and thousands of people at mission control in Houston went into action to save the crew from almost certain death. Fortunately, this was one drama which had a happy ending. The astronauts were returned safely to earth through the combined efforts of all the men and women involved in the space project.

As scientists, engineers, technicians, and astronauts evaluated the whole experience, they unanimously agreed on one point: "The crew was rescued because they *received* constant direction from mission control at Houston and *followed* that direction" (A. Theodore Tuttle, "Principles with a Promise," *1978 Devotional Speeches of the Year,* Brigham Young University Press, 1979, p. 1; italics added).

A critically important part of a pilot's training is learning the art of navigation, that is, learning how to chart a safe course using appropriate reference points. Set solar objects such as the North Star and the sun can be safely used as reference points.

The gospel of Jesus Christ is our North Star, or reference point, and Jesus Christ is the *Son* to whom we turn for proper light. God has set other lights (could we call them stars?) to be used as reference points to help us chart a safe course: the scriptures, living prophets, leaders and teachers, laws of morality and proper living, sacrament services and other Sunday meetings, as well as weekday instruction in seminary and institute classes. And, of course, each of us is blessed with the Light of Christ, which serves as our conscience. Members of The Church of Jesus Christ of Latter-day Saints have an additional reference point, the gift of the Holy Ghost.

In the same sense that natural reference points are sometimes obscured by clouds and stormy weather, gospel reference points are occasionally difficult to see. Satan provides shadows, eclipses, and darkness in an effort to subdue light and alter our course. It is difficult to remain on a strait course when mists of darkness dim our vision (see 1 Nephi 8:20–23).

Consider some of the devil's detours: dating before an appropriate age; poor personal grooming; viewing questionable movies, TV shows, or videos; listening to unwholesome music; missing Church meetings; necking and petting; experimenting with drugs, alcohol, or tobacco; reading trashy literature or viewing pornography; using profane and filthy language; failing to pray and read the scriptures. Each of these detours dim the light of the Spirit and lessen our chances for safe flights.

A classic example of how even minor alterations to a charted course can greatly alter the hoped-for destination is found in the following story by Elder Gordon B. Hinckley:

> Many years ago I worked in the head office of one of our railroads. One day I received a telephone call from my counterpart in Newark, New Jersey, who said that a passenger train had arrived without its baggage car. The patrons were angry.
>
> We discovered that the train had been properly made up in Oakland, California, and properly delivered to St. Louis, from which station it was to be carried to its destination on the east coast. But in the St. Louis yards, a thoughtless switchman had moved a piece of steel *just three inches.*
>
> That piece of steel was a switch point, and the car that should have been in Newark, New Jersey, was in New Orleans, Louisiana, *thirteen hundred miles away.*
>
> So it is with our lives—a cigarette smoked, a can of beer drunk at a party, a shot of Speed taken on a dare, a careless giving in to an impulse on a date. Each has thrown a switch in the life of a boy [or girl]

> that put him [or her] on a track that carried him [or her] far away from what might have been a great and foreordained calling. And as Nephi said, ". . . thus the devil cheateth their souls and leadeth them away carefully down to hell." (2 Nephi 28:21.) (*Ensign*, Jan. 1973, p. 91; italics added.)

Remember the lesson of the Apollo 13 flight! There was no room for a margin of error in their return flight from space. The slightest miscalculation or the least bit of resistance on the part of the crew to follow instructions would have sent them beyond their hoped-for target on earth, and their lifeless bodies might still be floating in the vast darkness of outer space.

In order to avoid Satan's shadows one must have his face directed toward the Son of God. When the light is on our face, the shadows are behind us. There is great significance in the Savior's emphatic statement, "Get thee *behind* me, Satan" (Luke 4:8; italics added).

Reflect upon the experience of the fourteen-year-old boy-prophet, Joseph Smith. When he first endeavored to call upon God in the Sacred Grove, Satan sought to destroy him. Joseph said:

> Thick darkness gathered around me, and it seemed to me for a time as if I were doomed to sudden destruction.
>
> But, exerting all my powers to call upon God to deliver me out of the power of this enemy which had seized upon me . . . just at this moment of great alarm, I saw a pillar of light exactly over my head, above the brightness of the sun, which descended gradually until it fell upon me.
>
> It no sooner appeared than I found myself delivered from the enemy which held me bound. *When the light rested upon me I saw* two Personages,

whose brightness and glory defy all description." (Joseph Smith—History 1:15–17; italics added.)

Note the significance of the words, "when the light rested upon me I saw . . ."! Light is of God. When we turn to the source of light, we see. Satan may attempt to duplicate light, but the difference between his counterfeit and the true light of God is very evident to those who keep their spiritual senses sharp.

Moses recognized the difference between God's true light and the devil's deception. When Satan comes tempting you to worship at his altar of sin, repeat the words of Moses: "Behold, I am a son [or daughter] of God, in the similitude of his Only Begotten; and where is thy glory, that I should worship [or follow] thee?" (Moses 1:13.)

There is great power in recognizing the truth in the phrase, "I am a child of God." Elder Gordon B. Hinckley offered the following observation: "That man who knows that he is a child of God, created in the image of a divine Father and gifted with a potential for the exercise of great and godlike virtues, will discipline himself against the sordid, lascivious elements to which all are exposed. Said Alma to his son Helaman, 'Look to God and live.' (Alma 37:47.)" (*Ensign*, Nov. 1975, p. 39.)

You are born of a truly royal heritage. Your heavenly parents—the King and Queen of the universe—have given you a heritage far superior to that which any earthly king or queen could give their children. When faced with temptations—choices that would drag you down to the dark side of life—remember the words often quoted by President Harold B. Lee: "Be loyal to the royal within you!"

Although all people on this earth are the sons and daughters of God, those who have taken upon themselves the name of Jesus Christ through the waters of baptism, becoming members of His Church and accepting the name of Latter-day Saints, have an even stronger responsibility to live up to royal standards. Reflect on the words of the Apostle Peter who said that the Saints of God are "a chosen generation, a royal priesthood, an holy nation, a peculiar [different from the world] people" (1 Peter 2:9).

There are thoughts, actions, words, music, associations, and environments that are simply below the dignity of one who is of royal heritage. Live up to your royalty. Figuratively speaking, you wear a crown of royalty. Do not allow your crown to become tilted or tarnished by surrendering to sin. The Lord has admonished us to "hold that fast which thou hast, that no man take thy crown" (Revelation 3:11).

When faced with temptation, hold fast to high standards. Echo the words of young Joseph who was sold into Egypt. He recognized his royal heritage and stood steadfast in spite of the tauntings and temptations he faced. His courageous reply to one who tempted him was: "How then can I do this great wickedness, and sin against God?" (Genesis 39:9.)

Your being born at this particular time in earth's history was not by chance. There was divine design in your birth. You have an important mission to perform that is part of the overall plan of our Father in Heaven. If you will let Him, God will take you by the hand and lead you in the paths you were expected to travel.

Consider the following comments made by two Church leaders:

> I believe that God has . . . chosen each young man and woman today for something of consequence in his grand design, . . . he loves you and he has a work for each of you to do (Gordon B. Hinckley, *From My Generation to Yours . . . with Love* [Salt Lake City: Deseret Book, 1973], p. 16).

> Do you think for a moment that Heavenly Father would have sent one of His children to this earth by accident, without the possibility of a significant work to perform? . . .
>
> . . . *You were preserved to come to the earth in this time for a special purpose.* Not just a few of you, but all of you. There are things for each of you to do that no one else can do as well as you. . . . If you let Him, I testify that our Father in Heaven will walk with you through the journey of life and inspire you to know your special purpose here. (H. Burke Peterson, "Your Life Has a Purpose," *New Era*, May 1979, pp. 4–5; italics added.)

It is vitally important that young people understand that they do not need to reach full maturity before they can chart a significant course in life. You need not wait to be married to be *worthy* to enter the temple. You don't have to wait to take seminary or institute classes to begin studying the scriptures. You need not wait to be called to go on a mission to teach the gospel both by word and example to your friends. You don't have to be mature in years to come to know your Father in Heaven and the Savior and to recognize and act upon the promptings of the still, small voice.

Nephi's brother Jacob beheld the glory of the Lord in his youth (see 2 Nephi 2:4; 11:3). Samuel spoke with the Lord when but a "child" (1 Samuel 3). Joseph Smith was called as a prophet at age fourteen. Mormon was entrusted with the sacred records of the Book of Mormon at age ten. President Thomas S. Monson was called as a bishop at age twenty-one and as an Apostle at age thirty-six. Countless members of priesthood quorum presidencies, bishoprics, stake presidencies, Relief Society presidencies, and Young Women leaders are currently being called while in their twenties to serve in these responsible positions.

Perhaps more important than anticipating a *future* call to serve, however, is a *current commitment* to excel in whatever your assignment may be. Be the very best deacon, teacher, priest, or member of your Young Women's class you can be. Whatever you are currently doing, strive for spiritual excellence now!

Remember, like the eagle, you have the potential to soar among God's heavens. Your divine nature is to become like our Father in Heaven and His beloved Son, who said: "Therefore, what manner of men ought ye to be? Verily I say unto you, even as I am." (3 Nephi 27:27.)

2

Magic Mirrors and Self-Esteem: Part 1

Mirrors play an important role in life. They assure that we more effectively apply makeup or are correctly shaven. They assist in keeping our hair in place and they can give quick feedback on our outward appearance, often helping to avoid much embarrassment.

Although mirrors may not lie, misplaced perceptions might cause distortions that can create lies. If, for example, a young woman is convinced that she is ugly, that her nose is too long, her hair the wrong color, her figure too thin or too fat, or her complexion something that resembles smashed strawberries, it doesn't matter what is really true, for in the mirror she will *see* only the negative image.

The boy who considers himself a toad will see nothing but warts staring back at him as he gazes in a mirror. Surely there is at least some semblance of truth in the saying that "beauty is in the eye of the beholder."

The following letter was once received by a personal advice columnist: "I am a sixteen-year-old girl who will come right to the point. I have never been asked out on a date by a boy because I have buck teeth. Can you help me? I hope so, because I am lonely and miserable and it's all because of my teeth."

What was this young girl's *real* problem? I can think of some pretty famous people, as well as many who are not widely known, who might give Bugs Bunny a run for his money in a contest for teeth of the year, but who have succeeded in spite of their protruding teeth. The girl's problem was not her teeth, but her negative attitude and her distorted perception about herself.

I recall reading once of a distraught young woman who referred to herself as a toad who wanted to be discovered by a prince and magically changed into a princess. She was fearful that she might be discovered by another toad and with a feeling of fateful resignation asked to share his lily pad for the rest of her life. Her problem was not only a misplaced personal perception but also a terrible distortion about how others looked as well.

Many people suffer from a modern variation of a dreaded disease that was common anciently—leprosy. While wandering in public the afflicted lepers were required to warn people of their presence by crying out, "Unclean! Unclean!" Those who are afflicted with the modern variation suffer from a low sense of self-esteem. They go around crying out, "Ugly! Ugly!"

How did people respond anciently when the lepers came along crying, "Unclean! Unclean!" They ran away or called them names. Some particularly unkind people even cast stones at the poor lepers. Unfortunately, people respond in much the same way today to those who constantly cry out, "Ugly! Ugly!"

A negative self-image is generally conveyed by a negative personality and often results in rejection and even ridicule by others. Negative people become prisoners in self-created confines that seem clearly marked with Keep Out, No Trespassing, and Beware signs.

"But," someone says, "suppose it really isn't my attitude that is the problem. Suppose I really do have warts on the end of my nose! Then what do I do?"

By measurements of worldly standards of beauty and bodily perfection, all of us undoubtedly come up short in some area. Little can be done about your height, skin color, size and proportion of body parts, and other things that genetics and heredity have bequeathed to you. However, some things can be done to improve your looks and overall attractiveness.

President Spencer W. Kimball once counseled a group of young people to take a personal inventory to see how they might improve their looks and personalities: "Take a careful inventory of your habits, your speech, your appearance, your weight, and your eccentricities, if you have any. Take each item and analyze it. Can you make some sacrifices to be acceptable? You must be the judge." ("There Is Purpose in Life," *New Era,* Sept. 1974, p. 7.)

As you take inventory of yourself, consider some of the following:

1. *Bodily cleanliness.* Do you bathe frequently and use appropriate soaps and deodorants?

2. *Oral hygiene.* Even though you brush your teeth regularly, are you sure your breath is not offensive? Do you need to use a mouthwash or breath mints?
3. *Grooming.* Is your hair clean and appropriately styled? Is your clothing clean and tastefully coordinated? Just as the jacket of a book gives a clue to the contents of the volume, so should your clothing make a clear statement about you.
4. *Personality.* Are you a smiling, friendly person? Do you reach out and try to make friends or do you wait for others to make the first move? Socrates prayed, "Make me beautiful within." People will overlook bodily defects if you catch their attention with a happy personality.

Rather than worrying so much about how others might react to you, how about concentrating on self-improvement? One poet gave this insight:

Does the flower fret
That the bee
Might forget
To buzz by?

Ah, no.
One concern
Has she,
And she tends
It well:
Her own smell.

(Carol Lynn Pearson, "To One Who Worries About Being Found," *Beginnings* [Salt Lake City: Bookcraft, 1985], p. 30.)

As we seek self-improvement, we should not become confused between conceit and true self-esteem. Elder Hartman Rector, Jr., suggested that "self-esteem is different than conceit—conceit is the weirdest disease in the world. It makes everyone sick except the one who has it. It is immensely important that you feel good about yourself." (*Ensign*, May 1979, p. 29.)

A prophet of God, President Harold B. Lee, gave the following counsel: "I recall the prayer of the old English weaver, 'O God, help me to hold a high opinion of myself.' That should be the prayer of every soul; not an abnormally developed self-esteem that becomes haughtiness, conceit, or arrogance, but a righteous self-respect that might be defined as 'belief in one's own worth, worth to God, and worth to man.' " (Conference Report, Oct. 1973, p. 5.)

Remember that God pronounced his creations "good," and that included you (see Genesis 1).

In response to the question as to what was the greatest commandment, the Savior said: "Thou shalt love the Lord thy God with all thy heart, and with all thy soul, and with all thy mind. This is the first and great commandment. And the second is like unto it, Thou shalt love thy neighbour as *thyself*." (Matthew 22:37–39; italics added.)

Appropriate self-love is simply a recognition of our relationship and obligation to our Creator. It involves an understanding of our divine origin and our divine potential.

With thoughts of pity, once from my heart I did cry,
"Magic mirror on the wall, who can be uglier than I?"

Then with a kind, but firm rebuke, methought I heard the glass reply—

"Thou canst be but mistaken for thy spirit is a child
born on high;
The offspring of so glorious a birth,
With a chance to improve thyself on earth.
Heavenly parents, with a beauty so exquisite, that I
cannot describe,
Look upon thee, their glorious creation, with unmitigated pride.
Nay, my child, thoughts of degradation in thee must
find no place;
For thou art a lovely creature, an offspring of God's
own race."

As I have pondered the lack of self-esteem, self-respect, positive self-image (call it what you will) that so many seem to experience, I have become convinced that these individuals simply do not understand their true nature as sons and daughters of Deity. How could we look down upon or speak evil of someone, including ourselves, who has the capacity to become like the Ones "whose brightness and glory defy all description" (Joseph Smith—History 1:17)?

Regardless of how limited you may presently consider your physical body to be, reflect upon these thoughts by Elder Sterling W. Sill:

> Now if you think it would be pleasant to be dressed in expensive clothing, what do you think it would be like sometime to be dressed in an expensive body—one that shines like the sun, one that is beautiful beyond all comprehension, with quickened senses, amplified powers of perception, and vastly increased capacity for love, understanding, and happiness. And we might just keep in mind that God runs the most effective beauty parlor ever known in the world. . . .
>
> . . . We have all seen plain people who have been made beautiful by the working of a radiant spiri-

> tuality. A godly spirit will make the plainest body beautiful. Great mental and spiritual qualities transform our bodies into their likeness. (*Ensign*, Nov. 1976, p. 48.)

Perhaps you have heard Max Beerbohm's story of George Hall, who had led an evil life and whose face reflected the sordidness of his character. To look upon him was to be repelled by his looks.

One day George met a beautiful girl named Jenny Mere. He was totally taken by her beauty and immediately proposed marriage. However, Jenny was the antithesis of George. She was not only outwardly lovely, but she was also beautiful from within. She told him that she could never marry a man whose face was so evil looking. She wanted to marry a man whose face reflected saintliness and love.

George was so taken by her beauty that he went to a famous mask maker, whose skill was such that he could completely hide a person's identity with a new, waxen face. The skillful mask maker fashioned the face of a saint over George's evil one, and when George looked in the mirror he saw reflected a face that Jenny could not resist. He knew that in addition to the new face, he would have to live the part of the saint if he were to truly convince Jenny that he was the man of her dreams.

George played his new role very effectively and won Jenny's heart. After their marriage, George continued to play the role of the saintly man, but he soon discovered that his love for his wife was such that he no longer had to act the part of a saint. He truly wanted to be good and his thoughts and actions were united toward this goal. Not only did he forsake his former life-style, but he actively sought ways in which to promote positive things in the lives of everyone around him.

By accident, his former friends found out his new identity. They came to him and urged him to return to his old ways. They were unconvinced that he was reformed and did everything they could to bring him back down to their evil level. When they did not prevail, they became angry and fell upon him with their fists. They tore the mask from his face and left him beaten upon the ground. They fled as Jenny came rushing from their small cottage.

Hiding his face in terror, George sadly contemplated the loss of the woman he so dearly loved. Surely, upon seeing his real face, she would be repelled in a mixture of horror and anger. The moment of truth had arrived! Gently tugging at his hands, fearing his face had been bruised and bloodied by the brutes who attacked him, Jenny looked into the face of this man she had grown to love.

Her reaction surprised George, for rather than revulsion he saw reflected in her eyes the same love and concern he had seen ever since he adopted the mask and his new ways. As they returned to the cottage and he looked in a mirror, George saw the miracle: line for line, feature for feature, his face had taken on the features of the mask. His actions had literally transformed him.

Although the story is fictitious, the lesson is real. President Spencer W. Kimball said: "There is no doubt that the life one leads and the thoughts one thinks are registered plainly in his face" (*Ensign*, May 1975, p. 81).

Another prophet of God, President David O. McKay, observed: "If we think noble thoughts; if we encourage and cherish noble aspirations; there will be that radiation when we meet people, especially when we associate with them. Every man, every person radiates what he or she is." (Deseret News Press pamphlet, *Saving the Family*, 1969, p. 20.)

In the Charles Dickens story, *Oliver Twist,* Dickens introduces us to a character named Monks, who starts as an innocent, beautiful child. Unfortunately, Monks allows himself to be swayed by things of a sordid nature, and his character undergoes a terrible transformation. At the conclusion of his life he was described as "a mass of solid bestiality, a mere chunk of fleshed iniquity. It was thinking upon vice and vulgarity, that transformed the angel's face into the countenance of a demon." (David O. McKay, Conference Report, Oct. 1951, p. 7.)

If you want a truly beautiful face, think beautiful thoughts. If you want a body that will someday be beautiful beyond description, live your life consistent with celestial standards. When the Apostle Paul spoke of celestial bodies, he was referring to the kinds of bodies that people of a celestial nature would inherit in the hereafter, for our resurrected bodies will reflect the kind of people we have become and the glory we will inherit (see 1 Corinthians 15:40; see also D&C 88:15–22).

If our days have been spent in doing good, then that is what shall be restored to us. If, on the other hand, our lives have been wasted in "sowing wild oats," we cannot pray for a "crop failure" at the last minute. Remember, "whatsoever a man soweth, that shall he also reap" (Galatians 6:7).

An ancient prophet has reminded us that if we have spent our days in doing good, we shall be raised to happiness in the kingdom of God, for good will be restored to good. On the other hand, if we have spent our time pursuing wrongful ways, we shall find ourselves in a state of misery outside of God's presence. (See Alma 41:3–6.)

Speaking of those who have spotted their lives with sin, Isaiah said: "The show of their countenance doth witness against them, and doth declare their sin

. . . they hide it not. Woe unto their soul! for they have rewarded evil unto themselves." (Isaiah 3:9.)

Self-esteem comes from knowing you are a son or daughter of our Heavenly Father with the inherited capacity to become as he is, and from acting accordingly. President Harold B. Lee counseled: "I would charge you to say again and again to yourselves, as the Primary organization has taught the children to sing, 'I am a child of God' and by so doing begin today to live closer to those ideals which will make your life happier and more fruitful because of an awakened realization of who you are" (Conference Report, Oct. 1973, p. 10).

Elder Gordon B. Hinckley added the following observation: "That man [woman, boy, girl, child] who knows that he is a child of God, created in the image of a divine Father and gifted with a potential for the exercise of great and god-like virtues, will discipline himself against the sordid, lascivious elements to which all are exposed" (*Ensign*, Nov. 1975, p. 39).

Look in your own magic mirror. See the reflection of one who has the potential to become fantastically beautiful and wonderful beyond anything imaginable. (Remember, Joseph Smith said that God and Christ were "beyond description.") It really doesn't matter if you have a few warts now, for just like the seemingly ugly wooly worm whose metamorphosis produces a winged creature of beauty, you, too, through tenaciously clinging to righteousness, can become a heavenly creature with a majestic body whose realm of travel will exceed the universe and whose possibilities are endless.

3

Magic Mirrors and Self-Esteem: Part 2

Now that you know who you are—a child of God—let's talk about some ways in which you can work towards having a greater feeling of self-esteem.

Reflect a wholesome, positive image. While it may sound crazy, have you ever thought of looking in the mirror and saying to yourself, "Hello, handsome!" or "Good morning, you beautiful person!" (You would want to make sure no one was watching you or they might try to convince you that you *were* crazy or conceited!) I am simply suggesting that you carefully avoid the *ugly disease* discussed in the last chapter. When you look in the mirror you should see a positive, worthwhile person smiling back at you. However, this cannot happen if there are unresolved thoughts and actions in your life that counter a godly spirit.

Elder Russell M. Nelson, of the Quorum of the Twelve Apostles, commented on mirrored reflections: "The first morning's glance in the mirror cannot reflect joy if there is any recollection of misdeeds the night before. The surest step toward joy in the morning is virtue in the evening!" (*Ensign*, Nov. 1986, p. 68.) Abraham Lincoln added this insightful observation: "It is difficult to make a man miserable when he feels he is worthy of himself and claims kindred to the great God who made him" (as quoted in Marvin J. Ashton, *Ensign*, Nov. 1976, p. 85).

Clean your personal closets of the clutter and cobwebs of sin. Counsel with the Lord and with your bishop regarding those mistakes that keep you mired in the muck of misdeeds. In other words, clean up your act! Keep yourself worthy, and you will feel good about yourself. And, as previously noted, you will reflect a more beautiful image. It doesn't matter what your past has been. The pages of your future are spotless and unblemished, but you must not endanger them by keeping alive pests from the past.

Accept yourself. It is all right to have role models to pattern some aspects of your life after—even the Savior counseled us to be like Him (see 3 Nephi 27:27). But it is important to remember that you are unique, an *original* made by God, and therefore you should not seek to become a carbon copy or a clone of someone else.

The following story, entitled "I Didn't Want to Be Me," illustrates the silliness of mimicking the habits and actions of another:

> All my life I didn't want to be me. I wanted to be like Harriet Wimpleton. So I walked like Harriet Wimpleton and I talked like Harriet Wimpleton. And then one day I noticed a strange thing—Harriet Wimple-

ton wanted to be like Connie Savorsen. She walked like Connie Savorsen; she talked like Connie Savorsen; and Connie Savorsen was walking and talking like Donna Heberson. And so here I was: walking and talking like Harriet Wimpleton's version of Connie Savorsen, acting like Donna Heberson; and guess who Donna Heberson was imitating—that pesky kid Wanda Droolson who walks and talks like me." (Author unknown.)

I recall hearing of a personal essay assignment given to third-graders. The youngsters were asked to respond to the question, "What do you want to be?" One child, who did not quite catch the teacher's intent but who was obviously possessed of positive feelings about himself, said, "I just want to be myself!"

As we view ourselves in relation to others, we could profit by considering the attitude reflected by Charlie Brown's dog, Snoopy. One day he sat on his haunches viewing the parade of people who passed by. He said to himself, "I wonder why some of us were born dogs while others were born people?" As he considered the matter, he concluded that the whole thing really wasn't very fair. His surprise punch line, however, was, "Why should *I* have been the lucky one?"

That is exactly how each one of us should feel about ourselves: "Why should I choose to be anyone else? I am really the lucky one. Let me discover and develop my own unique talents."

Avoid the "If only" pattern of self-defeating pity. How often have you heard someone lament his or her circumstances with the pitiful cry of, "If only?" "If only I had been home when he called!" (Perhaps some might say, "If only I had *not* been home when he called!") "If only I hadn't fallen down in the middle of the dance floor!" "If only I had not spilled my diet drink on her dress!" "If only I had ________!" (You fill in the blank with your regrets.)

The problem with "If only" is that it is backward oriented. Energy is needlessly wasted pining away about something that can't be changed. Elder Neal A. Maxwell has reminded us that, "Feet are made to move forward—not backward!" (*Ensign*, Nov. 1976, p. 14.)

The Apostle Paul gave us this wise counsel: "This one thing I do, forgetting those things which are *behind*, and reaching forth unto those things which are *before*" (Philippians 3:13; italics added).

At the 1960 Olympics, Cliff Cushman won a silver medal in the 400-meter hurdles, being only three yards behind the first-place winner. He appeared to be the prime candidate for the gold medal in 1964. However, he saw all the months of training, discipline, and even pain disappear in a split second as he tripped on a hurdle in the American trials. His fall eliminated him from further competition leading to the Olympics.

Cliff might have cried over how unfair he thought the system was and he might have relived in agony that moment when his foot hit the hurdle and he fell. He might have submerged himself in self-pity, crying, "If only I could have another chance!" However, Cliff was the kind of man who knew how to keep defeat a temporary situation and not allow it to continually clutter his future. Commenting on the incident, he said:

> But I tried! I would much rather fail knowing I had put forth an honest effort than never to have tried at all. . . .
>
> Certainly I was very disappointed in falling flat on my face. However, there is nothing I can do about it now but get up, pick the cinders from my wounds,

> and take one more step followed by one more and one more, until the steps turn into miles and miles into success." (As quoted in Elder William H. Bennett, *Ensign*, Nov. 1976, p. 31.)

What about you? Next time you get down on yourself because you feel you have failed at something, pick yourself up, wash the cinders from your wounds, and move on. You'll feel much better about yourself.

Compete with yourself. Remember the parable of the talents (see Matthew 25:14–30). Even though each individual had different talents, each was judged solely on the basis of what he had done. The Savior did not compare one with another. The man who was reprimanded received his rebuke because he had buried his one talent, not because he had fewer than someone else. We all have different talents, and we ought to be competitive with ourselves, not someone else. Your comparisons should focus on *your performance* as measured against *your potential.* Compete with the best that is within you.

Elder Marvin J. Ashton has counseled: "We must work each day to beat yesterday's record, not someone else's" (*Ensign*, Nov. 1974, p. 41).

I recall a Christmas carol about the donkey who sadly proclaimed, "I'm not beautiful, I'm not beautiful! What good to anyone am I?" His whole image changed when he discovered his value to Joseph and Mary as he carried the mother of the Christ child on her difficult journey to Bethlehem. By using the talents with which he was blessed, he came to see himself as a noble creature as beautiful as any other.

Glow through godly grooming. This is a way of saying, "Let your light so shine before this people, that they may see your good works and glorify your

Father who is in heaven" (3 Nephi 12:16). Reflect the light of the gospel in your grooming.

President Harold B. Lee noted: "Persons who are well groomed and modestly dressed invite the companionship of the Spirit of our Father in Heaven and are able to exercise a wholesome influence upon those around them" (*Speeches of the Year* [Provo: BYU Press, 1973], p. 92).

Not many years ago a highly educated woman sought to find God and his church but had been unsuccessful in her efforts to find either. One afternoon her doorbell rang and she opened the door to find two Mormon missionaries standing there. She said they were "dressed in suits, with white shirts and ties. Their hair was neatly combed. I was so impressed with them," she commented, "that I said: 'I don't know what you're selling, but I'll buy it.' "

Of course the missionaries were not selling anything, but they did have an important message to give the woman, and their appearance (their light) was so impressive that the woman listened, received the witness of the Spirit, and joined the Church. (See Conference Report, Apr. 1973, p. 75.)

Now, no one is suggesting that we all need to wear suits, white shirts, ties, or Sunday dress all the time. Nor do we need to wear the most fashionable and expensive clothing. We simply ought to look neat and clean, to look our best—to reflect godly grooming.

The prophet Alma counseled us to have "the image of God engraven upon [our] countenances" (Alma 5:19). I believe this includes godly grooming.

An Apostle of the Lord Jesus Christ, Elder Marvin J. Ashton, has offered these important insights regarding our appearance:

> Generally the cover or jacket of a book is designed to sell what is inside. We will not have to die

to be judged by the cover of the book of life. To those who would say, "It's what you really are inside that counts, not the length of the hair or beard," I would say, "If this is true, and I agree it is, why run the risk of looking like something you're not?" . . .

Self-image is often enhanced by the clothing worn. Appropriate, modest, flattering, and comfortable apparel helps a person feel good about himself. To be over-dressed or immodestly dressed may create wrong impressions and improper identification. Improper clothing may also lead to wrong actions. . . . We do ourselves and others a great injustice when we appear to be what we are not.

Reasonable questions to ask oneself could well be, "Can I be proud of my appearance? Do my clothes properly introduce me?" What better example of proper personal appearance can we have than that glorious introduction shared with us by the Prophet Joseph Smith when he declared, "I saw two Personages, whose brightness and glory defy all description" [Joseph Smith—History 1:17]. (*Ensign*, Nov. 1976, p. 84.)

Use wholesome language. An important element of proper self-esteem is the language you use. If profanity or filth is found in your mouth, how can you reflect a godly image? Vile and degrading language defiles and demeans the person who uses it and is an irritating pollutant to all who hear it.

On one occasion a rather loud, uncouth boy was using a barrage of filthy words in a lunch room. Although most of those whose ears were being assaulted by such profane pollution were offended, none seemed courageous enough to step forward and ask the boy to stop. Finally, one young man stepped up to the offender and pointing to the boy's mouth said, "How can you digest anything that has passed through *that* mouth? How do you dare process food through that garbage dispenser you call your mouth?" No more needed to be said. The message was clear and the garbage language ceased.

Would anyone willingly fill his mouth with filthy garbage? Yet, that is exactly what one does who speaks vulgar and filthy language. Such talk is appropriately named "gutter language." How can a mouth that profanes one minute seek to praise God in prayer at another time? How effectively can one seek help in a moment of need from Him whose holiness has been treated with such disrespect?

The use of foul language has reached epidemic proportions in much of our society today. It is heard in the schools, it is common in the entertainment media, and it is spoken in so-called high circles of society. Such an evil day was spoken of by ancient prophets and is the cause for alarm among modern prophets.

Elder Dallin H. Oaks, of the Quorum of the Twelve Apostles, has noted: "For many in our day, the profane has become commonplace and the vulgar has become acceptable. Surely this is one fulfillment of the Book of Mormon prophesy that in the last days 'there shall be great pollutions upon the face of the earth.' " (*Ensign*, May 1986, p. 49.)

Satan is having a field day listening to the language of hell as men and women, boys and girls, speak degradingly about body parts or functions and profane the sacred name of Deity. Have you ever thought that those who participate in this pollution are aiding the devil in his demeaning and demented desires?

President Gordon B. Hinckley has reminded us that those who resort to such language immediately show us that they are "poverty-ridden in [their] vocabulary" (*Ensign*, Nov. 1987, p. 48). President Spencer W. Kimball noted that "profanity is the effort of a feeble brain to express itself forcibly" (*Ensign*, Nov. 1974, p. 7).

Resolve to let your language be as the "tongue of angels," which the Book of Mormon tells us is the language of the Holy Ghost (see 2 Nephi 32:2). If you are living a godly life, your language will be clean, wholesome, and edifying. The Spirit will assist your speech. Such language will earn you the respect of people around you and, more importantly, it will please God and help defeat the devil's evil designs.

The importance of celestial speech to self-image was spoken of by Elder Marvin J. Ashton: "As important to our self-image and general conduct as appropriate dress, grooming, and hair standards are *moderation of voice, use of worthy language,* good manners, respect for others' rights, and courtesy" (*Ensign*, Nov. 1976, p. 85; italics added).

Think noble thoughts. Just as your language needs to be clean and wholesome, so do your thoughts and the things you allow to enter your mind. Surely, thoughts precede actions. President Ezra Taft Benson has noted, "Those who think clean thoughts do not do dirty deeds" (*God, Family, Country: Our Three Great Loyalties* [Salt Lake City: Deseret Book Co., 1974], p. 241).

While serving as president of Brigham Young University, Elder Dallin H. Oaks stated:

> Pornographic or erotic stories and pictures are worse than filthy or polluted food. The body has defenses to rid itself of unwholesome food. With a few fatal exceptions, bad food will only make you sick, but will do no permanent harm. In contrast, a person who feasts upon filthy stories, or pornographic or erotic pictures and literature, records them in this marvelous retrieval system we call a brain. The brain won't forget this filth. Once recorded it will always

> remain subject to recall, flashing its perverted images across your mind and drawing you away from the wholesome things in life. (*Ensign*, June 1974, p. 24.)

Occasionally, inappropriate thoughts come into our minds as uninvited guests. While we may not have had anything to do with their arrival, there is something we can do about their departure. Years ago, a faithful young missionary was serving honorably in his field of labor. However, he was troubled because he sometimes had thoughts enter his mind that were contrary to the spirit of his sacred calling. He was so conscientious about his work that he determined he could not continue to serve while being bothered by evil thoughts. To the delight of the devil, he decided to accept defeat and abandon his mission.

Before the young missionary could act upon his decision to leave his labors and return home, he attended a mission conference where President George Albert Smith spoke. President Smith gave an inspiring talk, bore his testimony, and began to return to his seat. However, before he sat down he returned to the pulpit. With great conviction he said, "The Spirit has indicated that I need to say something else. There are some of you who are troubled by your thoughts. Let me tell you that your mind is like a house and it has an entry way where an occasional uninvited guest steps through an open door. You may not have invited a thought to enter your mind, but you can decide whether to allow it to remain and make itself at home or whether you promptly throw it out and lock the door." The troubled missionary accepted the counsel and was able to complete an honorable mission.

There is a lesson to be learned in the Savior's story of the unclean spirit who was cast out of a man but later returned along with seven other wicked spirits to reoccupy the then vacant "house" (see Luke 11:24–26). If we do not occupy our thoughts with wholesome things, we leave the door ajar to uninvited guests. Elder Boyd K. Packer made this observation:

> Years ago I put up some signs in my mind. They are very clearly printed and simply read: "No trespassing." "No dumping allowed." On occasions it has been necessary to show them very plainly to others.
>
> I do not want anything coming into my mind that does not have some useful purpose. . . .
>
> I've had to evict some thoughts a hundred times before they would stay out. I have never been successful until I have put something edifying in their place. (*Ensign*, Nov. 1977, pp. 59–60.)

If you are to have a godlike character, a truly positive self-image that reflects the roots of your divine nature, you cannot afford to let the polluting pages of pornography, undesirable music, carnal comments from others, or sordid scenes from movies and television infect your mind. Be selective in what you read, view, and listen to.

The Lord has admonished, "Let virtue garnish thy thoughts unceasingly." Some of the promised blessings from acting upon this counsel are that your "confidence [shall] wax strong in the presence of God" and "the Holy Ghost shall be thy constant companion." (D&C 121:45–46.)

If you feel the presence of God in your life, having the Holy Ghost as your constant companion, you will be able to face any challenge and feel good about yourself. You will be able to look at yourself in the mirror and feel proud of the reflection you see.

Unlike the wicked stepmother of Snow White, you will never have to waste your time wondering "who is the fairest in all the land," for you will know what your possibilities are. You can rest assured that, ultimately, God will hold no celestial beauty pageant, for all who pay the price of living worthily will receive a body that will truly defy all description!

4

Daily Decisions Determine Your Course

The choices you make today set your course and determine the consequences of tomorrow. I remember hearing the story of a sixteen-year-old boy who, armed with his newly acquired driver's license, had been given permission to take the family car to a party. However, he was given the strictest instructions to be home before midnight. When it came time for him to leave the party in order to get home on time, he excused himself and tried to leave. However, several of his friends playfully barred his way, begging him to stay "just a few minutes longer." When the boy explained that he had to be home by midnight, one of the other party goers jeeringly said: "What's the matter, Cinderella, will your car turn into a pumpkin if you're not home when the clock strikes twelve?" "No," replied the boy, "it will turn into a bicycle, because that's all I'll get to drive for the next two weeks!"

Choices are rarely small and inconsequential. Your choice to watch TV today instead of studying for tomorrow's test will impact your future grade and perhaps to some extent your future opportunities for schooling, scholarships, and employment. Your decision to deny yourself some instant gratification now in favor of some future benefit will positively carve its mark upon your character as well as upon your future opportunities.

A former temple president and General Authority, Elder ElRay L. Christiansen, gave the following counsel to young people:

> It is your earthly life that you are now living, my young friends. You will live it but once. There will be no reruns, no repeat performances. What you are in this life determines where you will be throughout eternity.
>
> It is your future, your destiny that you are now molding.
>
> You made good in that pre-earth life. You were valiant there. You must not now "fumble the ball" on the twenty-year [or whatever your age is] line. When you do take the wrong course, you are undoing the work of your prior existence, for there you struggled for ages to prepare for mortality where you now are. (*Ensign*, May 1974, p. 26.)

To procrastinate—to wait until "tomorrow," "next week," or "when I get older"—changing a habit may be too late. Have you ever heard someone say, "Someday I am going to get my act together; be a happier, more friendly person; be more thoughtful of others; give up this bad habit; clean my room; properly prepare my school work; do things the first time I am asked; pay a full tithing; stop swearing; be on time and listen in my Church meetings; or do something I know needs to be done without being asked, even once"?

I recall seeing a Charlie Brown cartoon where frame after frame he sat slumped over his desk, agonizing over the idea that the teacher might call on him and he was unprepared. He tried to hide behind the student in front of him and silently, yet painfully, pleaded that he not be called upon: "Please, please don't call on me today." Just at the moment he thought he was doomed, the bell rang. As the relieved boy raced from the room, his friend Linus said: "Now you can go home and get prepared for tomorrow, right Charlie Brown?" To which the eternally procrastinating Charlie, having survived the current crisis of the day, replied: "Who cares about tomorrow. Come on, let's go play ball!"

During a period of pain, discomfort, or sorrow caused by some inappropriate action you have taken, have you ever resolved to change your ways if just given a second chance? But once freed from the troublesome situation, did you respond like Charlie Brown and concern yourself only with the needs of *now*?

Resolutions without commitment and follow through are worthless. They are futile exercises in rationalization. For without a true commitment to change, mistakes, tragedies, and sad scenes are simply repeated over and over again.

A Book of Mormon prophet reminds us of the importance of making positive changes now: "I beseech of you that ye do not procrastinate the day of your repentance until the end; . . . for that same spirit which doth possess your bodies at the time that ye go out of this life, that same spirit will have power to possess your body in that eternal world." (Alma 34:33–34.)

None of us know how long we will be upon the earth or how long our days of probation are. We grow up with the idea that we will pass through the various seasons of life and die at some point in our advanced years. For some, however, death comes as a surprise in an earlier season. Our challenge is to live each day to the best of our ability, for we never know which will be our last.

Consider the story of Gary and his bride, Frances. They had kept themselves worthy and qualified for a temple marriage and were married one sunny, summer day in the Salt Lake Temple. Five days later, while on their honeymoon, a tragic accident took their lives. However, while their "time" had been cut short, their "eternity" was in place, for their union had been sealed by the power of the holy priesthood. Their marriage was for "time *and* all eternity." (See "Couple Filled Life's Mission," *Church News*, Aug. 18, 1979, p. C-4.)

Although there was a tragic ending to their mortal lives, we can assume there was a happy ending to their celestial story. What if they had not been worthy of a temple marriage or had neglected to take advantage of this blessing? Under those circumstances their story would have had a very sorrowful ending.

Contrast the story of Gary and Frances with another young couple. This young man and woman had been taught the importance of a marriage that is sealed for time and all eternity and, like Gary and Frances, they too were very much in love. But for some reason they had not qualified for a temple marriage. Perhaps they rationalized, thinking that someday they would be *ready* to enter the temple, but for now they were content to settle for a marriage bound by civil authority.

Friends and relatives gathered as the starry-eyed couple exchanged vows, followed by a gala feast at their wedding breakfast. The wedding reception was to be held later that day in a distant city. However, it never took place. A car accident claimed their lives. Just three hours after their marriage for *time* was pronounced valid, death declared an ending to their union. Their short-lived marital bliss was broken as claim was made upon the fateful clause uttered under civil authority—"I now pronounce you husband and wife *until death do you part.*" Their marriage, which just a few hours earlier had begun with such happiness and high expectations, was now null and void in eternity. (See Spencer W. Kimball, "Marriage Is Honorable," *Speeches of the Year* [Provo, Utah: Brigham Young University Press, 1973], pp. 271–72.)

Obviously the daily decisions made by this young man and young woman, which had set the course of their lives on a path that led to a nontemple marriage, had a critical impact on their course.

Reflect upon the sad story of this young couple in light of these thought-provoking words by James Greenleaf Whittier:

> Of all sad words of tongue or pen,
> The saddest are these: "It might have been."

Remember, when you choose a certain course of action, you choose the consequences of that choice. Sometimes critical consequences come from careless choices that have been made without much forethought.

I once read about a native of the Amazon River region who suffered the consequences of being careless. From his infancy he had been taught that his survival in the jungle depended upon his being ever watchful for dangerous predators, piranhas, poisonous snakes, and plants. The man had been cleaning a chicken on the banks of the river and had thoughtlessly tossed the entrails into the water. Without considering the consequences, he dipped his hands into the murky water to wash off the blood. Instantaneously, he screamed and pulled his hands back—minus one finger which had been severed by the bite of a vicious piranha.

Youth, as well as those of all ages, cannot afford to be forgetful when it comes to spiritual guidelines and cautions. There are predators lurking all about you who will strike quickly if you become careless and let your guard down. The loss of a finger is inconsequential when compared to the spiritual damage that can be done to your soul through careless choices. Ultimately, the man's finger will be restored in the resurrection. However, if your choices close celestial doors, you may find it very difficult to reopen them.

Every decision you make should be carefully considered in light of its eternal ramifications on your eternal destiny. Some very simple insights on making choices were given by Moroni: "But behold, that which is of God inviteth and enticeth to do good continually. . . . For behold, the Spirit of Christ is given to every man, that he may know good from evil. . . . Lay hold upon every good thing." (Moroni 7:13, 16, 19.)

Perhaps the words of another Book of Mormon prophet, Jacob, and of a modern-day Apostle, would be an appropriate conclusion to this chapter on decisions and choices:

> O be wise; what can I say more? (Jacob 7:12.)

> Never [let] the needs of now crowd out the considerations of eternity (Neal A. Maxwell, *Ensign*, May 1976, p. 26).

5

Trivial Pursuits Versus Things That Matter Most

In recent years there has been great interest in amassing great hordes of knowledge of things of very little value and in playing games of trivia. The dictionary defines *trivia* as "unimportant matters: trifles." Something that is trivial is "of little worth or importance."

While there is good fun in playing games of trivia, there is danger in letting the acquisition of trivial facts assume a more important part in your life than it merits. There is an even greater danger, however, that some of your daily pursuits, which occupy a large portion of your time and energy and which you may not consider trivial, may in reality *be* trivial.

How are you using your time and talents? How about getting a piece of paper and writing down how you have spent the last twenty-four hours? How much of your time was spent in trivial pursuits as opposed to things that in an eternal perspective really matter most? You may want to keep a journal for a week—a time-log—in which you record the amount of time you spend eating, sleeping, watching TV, studying, talking with friends, serving others, earning money, attending school, exercising, or whatever you do. Divide your activities into two categories, trivial pursuits and those things that matter most. Analyze how you are spending your time. Ask yourself, "Am I satisfied with my current priorities or do I need to make some changes?"

It has been stated that too many people spend their lives climbing what they consider to be the ladder of success only to discover when they get to the top that it is leaning against the wrong wall.

Watch which walls you place your ladder against. Be certain those walls are clearly labeled. One of the things you can do to ensure that you pursue those things which matter most is to develop a personal mission statement about what you want to accomplish in life. Then set some short range and long range goals that will help you become what you want to become. Without such goals you will simply be tossed about on the surf of trivia and carried about by the currents of convenience. Without planning the direction you want to go in life you will be as the hitchhiker who carried a sign that read, "Anywhere!"

Among the areas of your life that merit your attention are physical, social, educational, and spiritual. Let's consider some aspects of these basic areas of concern:

Physical. What are you doing to maintain proper health? Remember, this marvelous machine we call a body requires maintenance and proper care just like any other machine of multiple moving parts. If it is abused or neglected, it will not run at peak efficiency and may break down before the originally intended warranty runs out.

Do you exercise regularly? eat properly? avoid harmful substances? get sufficient rest? "The condition of the physical body can affect the spirit," warned President Ezra Taft Benson (*Ensign*, Nov. 1974, p. 66).

Have you ever seen or read about an individual who was under the influence of alcohol or drugs? He does not have full control of his bodily and mental functions. We hear in the news almost daily the tragic stories of lives lost, bodies maimed, and characters scarred because of improper actions taken by one who was under the influence of these harmful substances.

Elder Boyd K. Packer has asked: "If someone 'under the influence' can hardly listen to plain talk, how can they respond to spiritual promptings that touch their most delicate feelings?" (*Ensign*, Nov. 1979, p. 20.)

The spiritual significance of the Word of Wisdom (see D&C 89) was noted some years ago by a member of the Quorum of the Twelve Apostles, Elder Stephen L Richards: "The Word of Wisdom is spiritual. . . . The largest measure of good derived from its observance is in increased faith and the development of more spiritual power and wisdom. Likewise, the most regrettable and damaging effects of its infractions are spiritual also. Injury to the body may be comparatively trivial to the damage to the soul in the destruction of faith and the retardation of spiritual growth." (Conference Report, Apr. 1949, p. 141.)

No one can afford to experiment with or try a harmful substance "just once." The potential damage to your mind, body, character, and spirit is too big a price to pay for a momentary thrill that is truly trivial. Make an irrevocable decision never to succumb to the temptation to taste such forbidden fruits.

Social. The words of God spoken in the beginning of this earth's existence still ring true: "It is not good that the man should be alone" (Genesis 2:18). You were meant to have friends and family. It is good to develop relationships with others.

Are you striving to make friends on a regular basis, or do you stick so close to a tightly knit clique that you may even appear to be unfriendly to others? This does not mean you should not have special friends, but don't limit your smiles and your conversations to just a few.

Do you make hasty judgments about others, not allowing yourself to reap the rewards of getting to know them? I can think of many friendships, and even some marriages, that started off with one or both individuals initially receiving a false impression about the other. Given time and effort, however, differences diminished and interest increased. Don't allow yourself to be "turned off" to another person's friendship because of some trivial thing.

One man who had previously had a problem in making snap judgments about others decided to change his approach. Instead of turning off all interest in someone he initially thought to be boring or uninteresting, he began to concentrate on them to discover what made them "tick." In the process he discovered that there were facets about their personalities that were fascinating. As a result he cultivated many new friendships.

Do you carry grudges or become bitter against those you consider your enemies, or do you seek ways to reconcile differences and bring peace to yourself and others?

During the height of hostilities in the Civil War, Abraham Lincoln made some kindly comments about the confederates. He was chided by a woman who thought Lincoln was carried away in his charity for the enemies of the Union. Her counsel was that he should concentrate more on destroying them.

Lincoln, as wise as he was compassionate, replied: "Madam, do I not destroy my enemies when I make them my friends?"

Cultivate the habit of courtesy. This is one of the greatest social skills you could develop. Courtesy is simply being thoughtful of others and being unselfish in your relationships with them. It involves respect and trust. Treat others in a manner that reflects their divine heritage.

Educational. What is your purpose in attending school? Are you taking advantage of your studies? Do your classes and your grades reflect favorably upon your future goals? Is your major focus strictly social? Is your time spent in trivial pursuits? Does your whole school experience revolve around the extra-curricular activities, most of which take place outside the class room? To the question, "What is your son taking up at college?" one disgruntled father replied, "Space!"

President Spencer W. Kimball gave this counsel to students: "Be serious about your studies. . . . Your minds need to be filled and stretched and trained. Adequate social opportunities are available, and these are important in terms of balance in your life, but do not subordinate your studies to the fleeting things of the moment." (*1980 Devotional Speeches of the Year.* Provo: Brigham Young University Press, 1981, p. 122.)

Grades are important not only in terms of their value as a measure of your performance in class but also as an indication of what you have learned and what you might be capable of doing. However, occasionally an undue amount of emphasis may be placed upon them. For example, a C+ or B- in a particularly hard course may be just as satisfying, because of the effort put forth to earn that grade, as an A in an easier course. Some people become paranoid about grades.

It is alleged that a man went into a Red Cross blood mobile for the first time to donate blood. Upon leaving, the donor was handed a card which identified his blood type and Rh factor. Glancing at the card, the novice donor said: "I don't understand. I was a good donor, my blood pressure was normal, I had no diseases, I didn't scream or faint, and all I got was a B-." Sometimes our best efforts don't pay off with high grades.

On occasion we expect more than we deserve. The story is told of one student who had not done particularly well in his studies. On the last day of class he left a self-addressed post card with his professor so that his final grade might be recorded and sent to him. At the bottom of the card the hopeful student cited the scripture from the Sermon on the Mount that states: "Blessed are the merciful" (see Matthew 5:7).

Several days later the student received the returned post card in the mail. The professor had penned the following message: "Blessed are they that mourn: for they shall be comforted. Final grade: D" (see Matthew 5:4).

Getting the most out of your school experience involves planned, continuous study. Too many students use what I call *revolving-door learning.* It is based on the principle that one should put forth the least amount of time possible in the long run while maximizing the use of the final hours before entering the door to take the exam. The consequence of this approach is almost total amnesia once one goes out of the door and leaves the classroom. Practicing this principle brings no lasting value, for even if the student is successful on the exam, the grade is no valuable ore mined through diligent study but merely fool's gold—appealing on the surface but essentially worthless.

The memorization of facts without an understanding of application is also a problem for some. Consider the case of the young man who had studied for a driver's test by memorizing the letters of the correct choices on a multiple-choice exam.

Later, when he experienced the reality of his car sliding on a slippery street, all he could think of was that the correct response to compensate for skidding was choice "c" on the multiple-choice exam. His shallow studying could not prevent his car from being crumpled.

We would all do well to learn from Nephi's approach to learning. He said: "I did liken all scriptures unto us, that it might be for our profit and learning" (1 Nephi 19:23). Could we not similarly say, "I will liken all my studies unto my daily life, that they might be for my profit and learning?"

Spiritual. While it is important to do well in secular studies at school, it is even more vitally important that your spiritual studies be an active and central part of your life.

Some years ago, while I was teaching at an Institute of Religion adjacent to a state university, a man in his midforties approached me outside of my office. He said, "Did Joseph Smith use a peep stone and a black hat to translate the Book of Mormon?"

I perceived that this really wasn't the issue that was troubling him, but responded by saying, "David Whitmer said he did. However, the Prophet's only statement regarding the translation was: 'Through the medium of the Urim and Thummim *I translated the record by the gift and power of God.*' " (*History of the Church* 4:537; italics added.)

I went on to point out that it didn't matter to me whether the Prophet translated by the Urim and Thummim—which consists of *two* seer stones—or by a single seer stone used with or without the hat described by David Whitmer. "The important point," I said, "is that however Joseph Smith translated the record, he did it under divine direction."

"Now the only way you can know for yourself if the translation is correct," I continued, "is to prayerfully read the book and seek the confirmation of the Spirit as to its truthfulness. That is the real issue to which you need to find an answer."

He responded by saying, "Oh, I read it when I was in high school. But I'm a lot more educated now. I have a doctorate and I don't believe in that stuff anymore."

I said to the man, "You know, when I was in high school I took a chemistry class. I haven't studied chemistry since then and my knowledge of the subject is severely lacking. If I were called upon to interpret a chemical formula or do an analysis of a substance, I couldn't do it. If you don't maintain your knowledge of a subject it becomes lost and worthless."

I bore my testimony to him of the truthfulness of the Book of Mormon and said, "I too have a doctorate, but I still have a testimony of the Book of Mormon because through continued study I have maintained close contact with that sacred book over the years. The Spirit still speaks to me of its truthfulness."

The prophet Jacob warned us about the foolishness of seeking the learning of the world and forgetting about God, for "it profiteth . . . not." However, he soundly pointed out that "to be learned is good if [we] hearken unto the counsels of God." (2 Nephi 9:28–29.)

It is important to seek learning. Your ability to adequately provide for yourself and those who will depend upon you for support in life will be largely contingent upon how well educated and how well skilled you become. However, as you pursue your secular studies take care that you don't neglect your spiritual studies. The Lord counseled, "Seek ye out of the best books words of wisdom; seek learning, even by study and *also* by faith" (D&C 88:118; italics added).

President Spencer W. Kimball once gave some interesting insights regarding that which matters most:

> The training we get in the universities, while excellent, is limited. It is but a very tiny percentage of the total knowledge. We encourage knowledge and its proper use, but we know there will be a thousand years to study about *things*, and as compared to the few years spent in universities, this great learning period is relatively limitless. . . .
>
> It is my understanding that when we have learned all we need to know about creation of worlds, that *we shall still need the power of the Priesthood to effect the creation.* (Ten-stake fireside address, Brigham Young University, Sept. 30, 1973, mss. copy, pp. 5–6; italics added.)

Speaking to a group of college graduates at their commencement exercises, Elder Boyd K. Packer gave the following counsel:

> It is not necessarily the education of the intellect that is the crowning achievement in life. It is time you learn, if you have not already, that there is a part of our nature, the part we term spiritual, that needs training as well. It is the spiritual part of our education that is most easily neglected.

> Consequently, we see many who are academic and intellectual giants but morally are puny 'and stunted and diseased. . . . It is the training of the spirit that strengthens the moral fiber of man. . . .
>
> Without a balance between the intellectual and the spiritual, we move through life without achieving real success.
>
> . . . Mortal life is a school, and most of the tests we undergo are multiple choice tests. If your growth in college has been solely intellectual, you may not have learned in the course of earning your diploma that the choice of life is not between fame and obscurity, nor is the choice between wealth and poverty. The choice is between good and evil, and that is a very different matter indeed.
>
> The sensors which assist us to make correct choices are only incidentally academic or intellectual. They are primarily spiritual. With balanced attention to each, you may have the best of both and then you will be educated. (*Church News*, June 19, 1983, p. C-4.)

Each of us came into mortality preregistered for the school of life. We gave our approval to the curriculum and the conditions for testing, grading, and the conferral of degrees that would be part of this school. In fact, you and I fought for the right to attend this school under its present administration. Each of us was given a unique contract. None would be graded on a curve where a predetermined percentage would have to pass or fail according to a hypothetical distribution of grades.

In God's school each will rise or fall, pass or fail, based upon *individual* performance rather than on group comparison. Although we may not now remember the details of our preearthly contract to attend this school, it is just as binding upon us now as the day we gave our assent to its being drawn up. None of us can become dropouts from this school of life, for even though we may fail to attend the required classes or complete the required course work, we remain registered and are still accountable for the assignments.

The required textbooks for your school are the scriptures. They are supplemented by inspired writings of Church leaders and constitute what could be called our celestial curriculum.

Your celestial curriculum is a vital part of your life. However, with the exception of regular instruction in established Sunday meetings and seminary or institute classes, your spiritual studies are basically self-initiated. You determine the amount of time you will spend searching and pondering the scriptures and the writings of prophets, Apostles, and other spiritual leaders. You will both assign and evaluate homework in these sacred texts. But the final grade in this celestial course will be assigned by the Master Teacher. Your performance will determine the degree (celestial, terrestrial, or telestial) you will receive on the Day of Judgment.

Do not cheapen the effect of your celestial curriculum by an overemphasis on trivial pursuits. Contemplate the things that, in an eternal perspective, matter the most. In the words of President Gordon B. Hinckley, "Cultivate the long view of your life" (*Ensign*, Nov. 1981, p. 40).

Relationships with Others

II

6

The Art of Being a Friend

What is the opposite of two? If you have a mathematical mind you may miss the answer. For the answer is not found in the exact sciences but in the social sciences. The opposite of two is a lonely me and a lonely you!

The Old Testament tells us that, "Two are better than one; because they have a good reward. . . . For if they fall, the one will lift up his fellow: but woe to him that is alone when he falleth; for he hath not another to help him up." (Ecclesiastes 4:9–10.)

Faithful friends are a source of strength. Friends are fun. Friends give comfort, cheer, counsel, encouragement, and, at appropriate moments, they warn us of dangers. True friends stand by us and help us become all that we are capable of becoming. They lift us to higher levels.

A young boy went with his lumberjack uncle to look for lumber. Spotting a gigantic tree standing alone in a clearing on a hill, the boy exclaimed: "Uncle George, look at that tree! It will make a lot of good lumber, won't it?"

The wise woodsman replied, "No, my boy, that tree will not make a lot of good lumber. It might make a lot of lumber but not a lot of *good* lumber. When a tree grows off by itself, too many branches grow on it. Those branches produce knots when the tree is cut into lumber. The best lumber comes from trees that grow together in groves. The trees also grow taller and straighter when they grow together."

Commenting on the truths reflected in this story, Elder Henry D. Taylor said: "It is so with people. We become better individuals, more useful timber when we grow together rather than alone." (Conference Report, Apr. 1965, pp. 54–55.)

It is important to have friends and to be a true friend.

Loneliness and rejection by others have caused much sorrow and many tragedies. In order to receive approval in a superficial way, some have turned to drugs, alcohol, bizarre behavior, people with low standards, and immorality. One girl who had sought acceptance through immoral behavior said: "Don't you understand what it meant to me to be needed by someone else, even if it was for just a few minutes of physical pleasure?"

For some the pain of loneliness is so severe that they have turned to suicide. Sometimes they really don't intend to take their lives but simply stage the suicidal attempt in a desperate plea for others to take notice of them. Sadly, the statistics of suicide deaths indicate that far too few have found the friendships they seek.

Some who seek attention would rather be noticed and rejected than ignored. The story is told of a criminal who walked into the post office and, upon seeing his picture on the wall, said, "Ah, it's nice to be wanted!" John Wolcott, an eighteenth-century writer, gave us this insightful verse: "What rage for fame attends both great and small! Better be damned than mentioned not at all."

What are you doing to reach out in friendship to others? Think about the people in your school classes or your neighborhood who need a friend? Wouldn't it be possible for you to go out of your way a little to make them feel worthwhile and wanted? You don't have to make them your *best* friend to make them feel welcome.

Some years ago, in a small high school, there was a young girl who was extremely heavy. She wore shabby, soiled clothing, and her hair looked like she had combed it in a blender. Because of her offensive odor, it was obvious that she didn't bathe very often. When she walked down the halls of the school it was like Moses parting the waters of the Red Sea—everyone just stepped aside. She was known for her voracious appetite and had even been seen snacking on spoonfuls of mayonnaise. As a result, she was named "Pig" by her uncaring classmates. Some boys would even mimic the snorting sounds of a pig as they walked behind her in the halls. She had absolutely no friends.

One day the school counselor met with the student body officers to talk about some special projects for the school. A number of things were suggested, most of them dealing with improving the physical facilities of the school and its surrounding area. A few suggestions involved some community service projects.

Finally, the counselor spoke up and said, "I have a very special project in mind. Why don't you make this the friendliest school in the state and begin by making Marie your friend!"

"Marie? Who's Marie?" the students asked.

"Would it help your memories if I mentioned the word 'Pig'?" the counselor replied.

Several of the boys said, "Oh, Pig! I didn't know she had another name." Then they started snickering, but soon stopped when they saw the seriousness of the counselor's face. The counselor went on to explain that Marie was a total reject in the school and that if she had some friends, if others were kind to her, maybe some of her bizarre behavior might change.

The students were ashamed of their actions and agreed that friendliness would become their special project for the year, with a particular emphasis upon Marie and others like her who seemed to be without friends. They began by saying hello to her in the halls. One of the student body officers was a big, strapping swimmer, wrestler, and football player. After he had a "friendly" discussion behind closed doors with several boys who had snorted at Marie in the hall one day, the word quickly spread that it was in the best interest of your health not to make fun of Marie or any other student.

Some of the girls worked with the home economics teacher to help Marie learn how to dress better, and they volunteered to work with the girl on class projects. They also suggested that the teacher deviate from her normal curriculum and have a special unit on personal grooming. Guest instructors came in and taught the girls how to take care of their skin and hair. Because Marie was not singled out as a bad example, but was simply part of the efforts of the entire class to improve their looks, she responded.

It took some time, but little by little Marie began to take pride in her appearance. She came out of her shell and began to return the now frequent greetings she got from most of the students in the school. The health teacher worked with her on a diet program, and the girl was asked to participate on some school committees.

By the end of the school year a miracle had taken place. No, she wasn't selected to the royalty of the Junior Prom, nor did she run for class office. But she did take pride in herself. She did have friends.

How would you like to be a miracle worker? In a sense, friends become great healers. In the next few pages are some suggestions on how you can be more friendly and join with others in a great circle of friendship.

Remember that all human beings are sons and daughters of God. Everyone you meet has a royal heritage. Treat each person with the dignity deserving of one who is the child of a King.

In the delightful book, *The Little Prince*, a rose is asked why she allows ugly caterpillars in her presence. She responded by saying, "Well, I must endure the presence of two or three caterpillars if I wish to become acquainted with the butterflies" (Antoine de Saint Exupery, *The Little Prince* [New York: Harcourt, Brace & World, Inc., 1971], p. 40).

Remember the story, *The Ugly Duckling?* The egg of a swan had mistakenly been placed in a nest of duck eggs, and when the tiny bird was hatched he was simply assumed to be a different-looking duck. He was laughed at, ridiculed, and rejected because he appeared to be so different from the others. None recognized him for what he truly was—a swan. As time passed, however, he underwent a marvelous metamorphosis and became the beautiful creature he was intended to be. Keep in mind that those you might now consider to be "ugly ducklings" have the potential to become celestial swans.

Treat others as people, not as things. You cannot establish strong relationships with others if you relate to them strictly in terms of something you hope to get from them. There is something painfully tragic about the line, "I'll be your friend (or allow you to hang around me) as long as you do something for me."

A friend is not something to be used and then discarded like some empty, disposable carton whose useful contents are gone.

Practice being friendly. Have you ever been on an elevator when others got off, leaving just you and one other person standing on the same side of the elevator? What did you do? What did the other person do? It is likely that one of you moved to the other side of the elevator. Then, for the remainder of the ride, you probably focused your gaze upon the little box that shows the floor numbers. You probably did not speak to one another. Why?

Have you ever been walking down the street, or a hallway, and passed someone you did not know? Where did you focus your eyes? Generally speaking, most people turn their gaze away from the person they are passing. Like two passing automobiles, the passing people dim their lights until the coast is clear. Why do people avoid being friendly?

Discomfort and fear of rejection are two reasons that people avoid approaching others. Have you ever greeted another person only to be snubbed? It does happen. However, why allow your fear of an encounter with a grouch to prevent you from having some very positive experiences and even making some new friends?

I had a really interesting experience on one occasion. I was in a shopping mall and caught the eye of a man coming the opposite direction. He looked familiar, but I couldn't remember his name. As we got closer I saw that he was looking at me as if he knew me. We stopped and exchanged greetings, inquiring how each was and had a pleasant little visit. Finally, I said, "I'm sorry but I just can't remember your name." He then told me his name, but it didn't ring any bells of recognition in the recesses of my memory. He then apologized to me that he had forgotten my name. I told him my name, and he too drew a blank from his memory bank. We discovered we didn't know each other at all. However, we had enjoyed a few minutes of conversation and parted with a smile and the comment that it *really* was nice talking with, and meeting, each other.

Why not try setting a goal for yourself that you will say "hello" to, smile at, or introduce yourself to a given number of people during the next few days. It may be a little hard at first but you will find some real dividends and it will be fun. You will probably find people who have been wanting to get to know you but were afraid to take the first step.

The Bible gives us this sound counsel: "A man that hath friends must show himself friendly" (Proverbs 18:24).

Concentrate on the other individual and forget yourself. You will make friends by being genuinely interested in others, not by trying to get others interested in you. I recall hearing a psychiatrist once say that fewer people would be screaming, "Notice me! Notice me!" if they concentrated on service to others.

Avoid labeling, name calling, and cutting com-

ments. A grown man once told a group of teenagers one of his biggest regrets in life. Although it had been thirty or forty years since he was in elementary school, he was still troubled by his participation in cutting down a classmate.

There was a girl in his second grade class who was a little different than the rest of the boys and girls in the class. She didn't wear very good clothes. Her hair was kind of stringy looking and she wasn't very sociable. She also seemed to be absent from school a lot.

Somehow she was given the name of "Stinky Sorensen" by her cruel classmates. They didn't use the name to her face, and they didn't openly make fun of her, but whenever they talked among themselves she was referred to as "Stinky." Nobody wanted to sit by her and everybody avoided even touching her. She was treated as if she had a disease.

The man telling the story said that he did not know what ever became of her. He couldn't remember her in the later grades of his elementary school. He said he had concluded that a major reason why the girl was absent so often was that she couldn't take the rejection she received from those who should have been her friends.

The next time you feel inclined to cut someone, think of what that means. You are *wounding* another with your words. Consider the consequences of your thoughtless actions:

> Boys flying kites haul in their white-winged birds;
> You can call back your kites, but you can't call back
> your words.
> "Careful with fire" is good advice, we know;
> "Careful with words" is ten times doubly so.
> Thoughts unexpressed will often fall back dead.
> But God Himself can't kill them, once they are said!
>
> (Will Carleton, *The First Settler's Story.*)

We could do well to follow the example of a Wyoming woman who was known as "the defender of the absent." It seems that when she was in a group and cutting comments were made about someone who wasn't there, she always inserted something positive about that person. As a result of her positive approach to people, she never lacked for friends.

People often act like a pack of chickens. When one chicken has a sore or a wound on its body, the other chickens gang up on the sick chicken and peck at its sore. This prevents it from healing and, if untreated, will result in the death of the harassed bird. It takes courage to avoid joining the crowd in pecking at one who has been wounded with words.

Be a builder of others, not a destroyer. I recall how excited I was as a young boy when my neighbor hired me and several other of my friends to tear down his double garage. I thought it was great fun to wreck something not only with someone's approval but also to get paid for it in the process. Because of the deteriorated condition of the garage, we accomplished our task in one day. When my dad came home from work I proudly displayed my pay and told him what we had done. Then I said, "I think that is what I want to do when I grow up. I'm going to be a wrecker."

My father offered a wise observation which I have never forgotten: "Anybody can tear something down," he said, "but it takes somebody special to build something up." Consider the implications to people: anybody can tear somebody down, but it takes somebody special to build another up.

Look for ways to praise another honestly. We are not talking about false flattery, which is the devil's counterfeit, but about genuine, deserved praise. Someone once said that to praise another is an investment in happiness. Oliver Wendell Holmes is credited with having said: "Friendship is the pleasing game of interchanging praise." Invest in the warm sunshine of praise. It brings lasting profits.

Respect differences without condoning wrong conduct. Be one who always looks for the positive in another. You don't have to condone wrong conduct but neither do you have to be the first one in line to throw stones. The Savior taught us a lesson about this (see John 8:1–11).

Elder Neal A. Maxwell once related this sage advise: "A wise lady once said that what we hope our friends will do is to separate the wheat from the chaff and, with a breath of kindness, blow the chaff away. I am grateful now, as I have been over the years, for friends who have had strong lungs." (*1976 Devotional Speeches of the Year* [Provo, Utah: Brigham Young University Press, 1977], p. 188.)

I recall Elder Paul H. Dunn telling the story of how he was attending a convention of great athletes. One of them, a Baseball Hall of Famer, spoke at the convention but used such foul language that Elder Dunn decided to take some action. When the man sat down Elder Dunn told the star that as a young boy he had really admired him. "You were my idol and I had you on a high pedestal," he said. But then, showing his true friendship, Elder Dunn added, "But tonight you fell off that pedestal." He explained how offended he was at the man's profane language and then said: "I'm going to challenge you tonight, as your friend, to clean up your language." (See *Ensign*, Nov. 1976, p. 55.)

Elder Richard L. Evans has given us this sound counsel:

> One of life's most important problems is learning to get along with the people with whom we live in the world, without compromising principles. . . . It is quite impossible to do everything everyone else

> wants us to do or to please all people, because everyone else wants us to do something different, and abandoning principles is no solution to the problem of getting along with people. . . . *Compromising principles isn't getting along with people; it is simply surrender,* . . . We lose face and deceive ourselves when we seek supposed popularity or the supposed approval of other people at the price of principles. (Conference Report, Apr. 1959, pp. 123–24.)

Those who will desert you because you fail to abandon the principles *they* have forsaken are not true friends.

Avoid "I" trouble. I recall reading a letter from a forlorn young teenage girl who complained that she had no friends. In her short letter she had focused entirely upon herself and her assets. Never once did she inquire about how she could be of service or a friend to others. She simply wanted everyone to come her way. She really had "I" trouble.

This principle was well illustrated in a Charlie Brown cartoon some years ago. Lucy was seated on the floor in a state of self-pity, wondering if someone was ever going to love her and if she was going to have friends who really liked her. Charlie's faithful and lovable dog, Snoopy, was seated close by listening to Lucy's lament. He puckered up and said, "Look right here, Sweetie, I like you." But Lucy was so caught up in her self-pity that she didn't see him leaning towards her. He finally fell flat on the floor, bruising his nose in the process. The final frame showed Lucy still lamenting, "No one is ever going to like me," to which Snoopy, rubbing his sore nose, replied, "You're probably right, Sweetie!"

A woman once approached one of the General Authorities who was visiting at her stake conference and complained that she had lived in the area for four months and nobody had visited her. Expecting a sympathetic response and, perhaps, even a slight rebuke for her neighbors, the woman was surprised with the response: "In that four months how many people have you visited, Sister?" You see, the General Authority put the responsibility right where it belonged, squarely on the shoulders of the woman. True, others should have made an effort to visit her, but none of us can afford to sit back and expect others to always make the first move. We must take the initiative.

Avoid getting too busy to notice other's needs. Jesus was a classic example of a person who was sensitive to others' needs and to their presence. He noticed Zacchaeus perched high in a tree, away from the crush of the crowd (see Luke 19:2–9). He alone was aware of the woman who secretly touched the hem of His garment in hopes of receiving a healing (see Mark 5:25–34). He was very much aware of the individuals who needed His attention in spite of the throngs who pressed on Him and the many demands on His time.

A very sensitive surgeon was not too busy to notice the needs of a little boy who was awaiting surgery. The child clung desperately to a battered, one-eyed teddy bear which the nurses had tried unsuccessfully to remove from his sterile bed. Sensing what needed to be done, the doctor said: "That's all right, leave Teddy there. He needs some surgery too!" The child relaxed and willingly submitted to the anesthesia.

When the small boy awoke he immediately looked for his furry friend and discovered that Teddy was snuggled right next to him on the pillow—with a skillfully placed surgical bandage across his missing eye.

Forget your own discomfort and think of others. Perhaps this is another way of saying: view friendship as an opportunity to give rather than to receive. In writing to the Latter-day Saints, the Prophet Joseph Smith once said: "I am, as ever, your humble servant and never deviating friend" (D&C 128:25).

One man who used to have a fear of entering a room full of people found a way to overcome his problem. He would pause before entering the room and survey the situation, looking for some way he could make the room more comfortable for someone else. By focusing his attention on others, he lost his fear.

Practice being a friend with your own family. What better friendships should you have than with members of your own family? If you are kind, courteous, pleasant, and helpful with members of your own family, these same traits will come naturally when you deal with others.

Two young boys were observed riding full speed on their bikes down a street. The first had a bag of newspapers attached to his bike, and, as he reached the corner, he was unable to negotiate the turn and crashed, spilling his papers all over the road. The second boy rode by without breaking speed, but laughing wildly at the misfortune of the first.

A neighbor came out to help the newspaper boy pick up his papers and see if he was all right. The man said, "Your friend was not very nice in not stopping to help you," to which the boy replied, "He's not my *friend*, he's my *brother*!"

Contrast this boy's experience with that of a young girl named Debbie, as related by Elder Vaughn J. Featherstone:

> "I want to tell you about a friend I had when I went through high school." She said she felt homely, but her friend told her she was beautiful. When there were dances, he would dance with her. He built her

up. She said: "He was my very best friend. He was handsome and popular, and he lived his religion. I never heard him swear, he never violated the Word of Wisdom, and he faithfully went to church.

"It was a good thing that he was a strong member of the Church," she said, "because I tailed him everywhere he went. I did what he did, and I would have followed him anywhere. I cannot express the love and respect I have for him. I was not his girlfriend, but I sure loved him. He is on a mission now, and we write regularly. He still loves me and is still my best friend. He is my older brother." (*Ensign,* Nov. 1987, p. 28.)

Place your welcome mat in plain sight and operate on the smile principle. Have you ever walked up to the door of a house you have never been to before and felt a little discomfort in knocking or ringing the door bell because you weren't quite sure what to expect? Didn't you feel a little better if you saw a door mat that said, WELCOME! A welcome mat is a sign of friendliness on the part of the inhabitants of the house. On the other hand, signs that say KEEP OUT certainly give some indication of the kind of reception you might receive if you choose to ignore the sign.

People actually display similar signs around themselves. By your actions, the look on your face, and the tone of your voice, you are displaying either a WELCOME sign to others, inviting them to enter your circle of friendship, or you are displaying a warning sign that says KEEP OUT! Sometimes a negative sign is hung out without a person realizing it, but, intentional or not, its effects are the same—others shy away from trying to be friendly.

One of the best places to hang out your welcome mat is on your face. There is strong truth in the fun little song which says, "No one likes a frowning face, change it for a smile. Make the world a better place by smiling all the while." Maybe the world would do well to follow the lead of a law passed in Pocatello, Idaho, many years ago which simply said it was illegal for anyone to go around "looking peeved or dejected." Joseph Addison once said, "What sunshine is to flowers, smiles are to humanity."

Did you know that it takes fewer facial muscles to smile than it does to frown? A smile is such a simple investment that pays such great dividends. A happy, friendly smile is very catching. It is hard to resist smiling when you see someone else smile. Do your part to clean up the pollution of gloom. Smile!

Clear your closet of clutter and your guest room of unwanted guests. Do you have any of the following cluttering up the closets of your mind or making themselves at home in your mind's guest room? Miserable memory? Terrible trifles? Painful past? Wrongful rejection? Unwanted unhappiness?

If you allow any of these things to remain, constantly entertaining them, you make it very difficult for happy thoughts to enter your mind. Don't allow a real or imagined wrong or slight from someone else to continue to hurt you by constantly dwelling upon it. There is healing medicine in forgiveness. Carefully consider the counsel contained in the Book of Mormon that "a bitter fountain cannot bring forth good water" (Moroni 7:11). How can you possibly be a happy person if you harbor unhappy or unkind thoughts?

Elder Marion D. Hanks related the lesson of a rattlesnake bite that is very applicable to the course of action one should take when hurt by another: "There are two courses of action to follow when one is bitten by a rattlesnake. One may in anger, fear, or vengefulness pursue the creature and kill it. Or, he may make full haste to get the venom out of his system. If he pursues the latter course he will likely survive, but if he attempts to follow the former, he may not be around long enough to finish it." (*The Gift of Self* [Salt Lake City: Bookcraft, 1974], p. 295.)

Why not start today, right now, to be a more friendly, forgiving, caring person? As you reach out to others you will find great satisfaction. A person who is seeking the welfare of others is not a lonely or miserable person.

Elder Gordon B. Hinckley summed up the essence of friendship: "Sacrifice, service, decency, goodness, helpfulness—these are the basis of friendship" (*From My Generation to Yours . . . with Love* [Salt Lake City: Deseret Book, 1973], p. 26).

7

Popularity and Peer Pressure

It is normal to want to belong. It feels good to be liked and needed. No one wants to be rejected or left out. There is nothing inherently wrong with wanting to be part of a group, for a man is a social being. As previously mentioned, God's words ring true: "It is not good that the man should be alone" (Genesis 2:18).

There is strength in uniting with another. Marriage is an example of such strength, with the joining of a man and a woman in an eternal companionship. Missionaries are sent out "two by two." Bishops, presidents of stakes, leaders of auxiliaries, and priesthood quorums all serve with counselors. Even the prophet has counselors at his side. God himself does not operate in a social vacuum. His beloved Son and the Holy

Ghost are members of the Godhead, and they are surrounded by myriads of heavenly beings who assist them.

Feeling alone and left out can lead one to despair and even panic. Consider the battle of Missionary Ridge during the Civil War. Just outside Chattanooga, Tennessee, a numerically superior force of Confederate soldiers held the ridge. They seemed invincible to any attack from Union troops. Yet, they were defeated and the ridge was lost.

Why had their advantage not proven effective?

An analysis of the battle showed that the Southern soldiers were spread so thin and were so isolated from one another that they felt alone. They could not hear the supportive voices of their comrades or their leaders amidst the roar of battle. Panicking, they deserted the security of their positions and surrendered to the oncoming Northern troops.

It is good to be surrounded by strong, supportive friends and family. We need to hear voices of encouragement. Without such support, many have panicked in moments of loneliness, compromised their positions, left the safety of their values, and surrendered to sin.

However, while strength can come in numbers, weaknesses can also be found in the companionship of the wrong individual or group. Some mistakenly seek strength in popularity. There is potential danger in wanting to be part of the so-called popular crowd.

The dictionary states that popularity implies being widely *accepted*; commonly *liked* or *approved*; being held in *regard* or *favor* by others. You will note that this definition makes no mention of virtue, rightness, goodness, or morality. If the price of popularity is at the expense of proper values, the price is too high.

The *in* group may really be *out* of it as far as God is concerned.

When pressured by our peers to do something we know is wrong, no matter how *popular* it may appear to be, our answer can be no less than that of a young man who resisted similar pressure many years ago, "How then can I do this great wickedness, and sin against God?" (Genesis 39:9.)

Every time we are pressured by someone to "join the crowd," it would be well to remember the following counsel from Elder Richard L. Evans:

> There is something formidable called crowd psychology, when many seem to move compulsively, not necessarily having thought things through. And one of the urgent lessons to learn is that *a wrong isn't right just because many do it.* A wrong isn't right just because a crowd does it. And no member of a crowd is relieved of personal responsibility when he does with others what he wouldn't do himself. A crowd is composed of individuals, and basically its acts are the acts of individuals. And before a boy or a girl does something he shouldn't, takes something he shouldn't, uses something he shouldn't, behaves as he shouldn't, in a crowd or with other company, he ought to pause and ask himself honestly: "Would I do this if I were alone, if I were thinking my own thoughts, and considering the consequences, without the compulsion of other people?" ("In a Crowd," *New Era*, Feb. 1971, p. 18; italics added.)

One of Satan's most effective big lies is the phrase "everybody is doing it." The insidious insinuation is that if you are not "doing it" you are "strange," "different," "weird," "not popular," and "out of it." Bishop Glenn L. Pace has counseled: "Don't be fooled by the argument, 'Everybody's doing it.' Your spirit should be offended and your intelligence insulted by such reasoning." (*Ensign*, Nov. 1987, p. 40.)

I recall one of those occasions when my spirit was offended by the *big lie.* I was watching a news program when a reporter interviewed some famous (or should we say infamous) rock stars who were going to perform at a local concert. This group was known for its use of drugs. In an attempt to justify his continued use of these harmful substances one of the performers said: "Well, everybody tries drugs at some point in their life but some just graduate to regular use." Such a self-serving statement is simply not true! There are many, many wise and noble young people as well as those of an older generation who have not succumbed to such self-abuse of their minds and bodies. Don't fall for this snare of Satan!

A good point to remember is that one does not have to follow the crowd, indulging in its perverted practices, in order to be respected and liked. At a time when the moral fabric and values of the entire Nephite civilization were crumbling, a teenager named Mormon, who stood firm in his faith and principles, was selected as the leader of the nation's armies (see Mormon 2:1–2).

President David O. McKay said: "Indeed men who yield to temptation to seek popularity among friends lose the very thing they desire, while the boy who maintains his standards wins their respect" (*Church News*, Oct. 23, 1965, p. C-16).

One of the keys to maintaining the respect and admiration of others is to be consistent in your behavior. Others must know that you are not wishy-washy and cannot be swayed according to the pressure of the moment or the masses. Dr. David P. Gardner, former president of the University of Utah and now the head of the multiple-campus University of California, gave the following counsel:

> As I was growing up in Berkeley, I found that it was not necessary for me to abandon my own beliefs or pattern of life in order to live happily with others. No one insisted upon it. It was necessary for me to adapt or accommodate my own behavior to what was the accepted norm of the time. It was not necessary to do that. It was necessary, however, that I be consistent in my behavior. One cannot take a drink under certain circumstances and then refuse to do so under others. One cannot live that way. If one is consistent, one will be respected.
>
> There is, of course, an enormous difference between respect and popularity. The former has an enduring and sustainable character to it. The latter is transitory and fleeting. ("On Living," Salt Lake Institute of Religion Devotional, Nov. 4, 1977, p. 6.)

The fleeting nature of popularity can be seen all around you. The athlete who is cheered for his feats today may be jeered for his mistakes tomorrow. Many a popular beauty queen or rising Hollywood star has faded into obscurity. Politicians who seemed at the pinnacle of success have seen their popularity fade at the polls. Terrestrial and telestial popularity is terribly tenuous.

On the other hand there are those who were not particularly popular in their day who are numbered among the greatest who have walked the earth. Noah was undoubtedly considered to be a little crazy by his neighbors. The day *before* the flood his popularity profile was probably at a very low ebb. However, the day *after* the flood began Noah might have won an election quite handily—*if* there had been anybody left to vote.

The prophet Lehi was not well accepted among the ancient inhabitants of Jerusalem. He was ridiculed by the crowds and some even sought to take his life. (See 1 Nephi 1:18–20.) Another Book of Mormon prophet, Samuel the Lamanite, was similarly belittled and threatened by the crowds. His skin was not the *in* color among the Nephites and his message was very unpopular. (See Helaman 13–15.) Yet both of these prophets will stand in eternity among the noble and great to whom all things shall be given, while their detractors will fade into obscurity in lesser kingdoms.

A more recent prophet, Joseph Smith, was similarly not very popular in the world's eyes. While he was still a young man, a heavenly messenger prophesied that Joseph's "name should be had for good and evil among all nations, kindreds, and tongues" (Joseph Smith—History 1:33). During his short life he was constantly maligned and persecuted. Dozens of unfounded law suits were filed against him and he was falsely imprisoned. While enemies sought his life, some so-called friends betrayed him. Following his martyrdom there were those who tried to tarnish his memory. And to this day there are those who seek to vilify his character. But all of this avails nothing, for he stands rock solid as one of the greatest men to have lived (see D&C 135:3).

What about the Savior? How well did He fare in the popularity polls of his day?

His flawless character was assailed with such epithets as "a gluttonous man, and a winebibber, a friend of publicans and sinners!" (Luke 7:34.) He was accused of having a devil (see John 8:48), and there were those who attempted to stone Him (see John 8:59). He had former friends and disciples who "walked no more with him" (John 6:66). Among those who turned away were some who knew of the correctness of the Savior's teachings but who feared for their positions in society: "For they loved the praise of men more than the praise of God" (John 12:42–43). A trusted friend betrayed Him with a kiss (see Luke

22:47–48) and another denied Him (see Luke 22:54–62). He was mocked, buffeted, and spat upon by some for whom He had so recently suffered in Gethsemane (see Matthew 26:67–68). In a vote of *popularity* between the sinless Son of God and the criminal Barabbas, Jesus was rejected and consigned to suffer death on the cruel cross (see Matthew 27:15–26).

When you are ridiculed, laughed at, and rejected for refusing to give in to popular pressure, remember the words of Him who paid such a terrible price to provide the Atonement for you: "If the world hate you, ye know that it hated me before it hated you" (John 15:18). Then, too, remember that the day will come when at the mere mention of His holy name every knee shall bend and every tongue confess Him as the Savior (see Philippians 2:9–11).

Elder Hugh B. Brown, who served as an Apostle—a special witness for the Savior—made this observation: "The value of approval depends on who gives it. Sometimes I am not satisfied because of the people who approve." (*Eternal Quest* [Salt Lake City: Bookcraft, 1956], p. 436.)

When you make a wrong choice, Satan smiles with sneering satisfaction. But when you choose to stick to correct principles and values, resisting pressure to compromise standards and give in to the crowd, you receive divine approbation. Perhaps you will then feel what the Nephites experienced when "Jesus blessed them . . . and his countenance did smile upon them, and the light of his countenance did shine upon them" (3 Nephi 19:25).

Some basic questions to ask yourself when pressured to make any choice are these:

1. Is it right? (The popularity of the world is generally based on expediency and what is

known as situational ethics, which simply states the false doctrine that there are no absolute values.)
2. Will it make me a better person?
3. Will it lift and make others better?
4. Will my Father in Heaven and the Savior approve?
5. Will my choice draw me closer to Christ, who seeks my well-being, or to Satan, who seeks to make me as miserable as he is (see 2 Nephi 2:18, 27)?
6. Would it embarrass my parents and my family?
7. Would I be embarrassed to have my decision shown on public television?
8. Will this choice bring me true happiness or merely short-lived pleasure?

Even though your choices may be correct, there will always be those mocking masses occupying the "great and spacious building" who will point their fingers at you and ridicule your courage with taunts of "chicken," "momma's boy," "square," "nerd," "dud," or some other cutting comment meant to dissuade you from the right course (see 1 Nephi 8:26–27).

Reflect upon the reaction the sons of Mosiah received from some of their so-called "friends" when they announced their intention to serve a mission. Their friends "laughed [them] to scorn" (Alma 26:23). Yet the sons of Mosiah stuck to their resolve and served their mission. They had great success in changing the lives of others for the better, in addition to improving themselves because of the impact their missionary experience had on their own lives.

A more recent example of a righteous individual being "laughed to scorn" involved a young beauty queen who held high standards. In 1966 a lovely Latter-day Saint named Dianna Lynn Batts was touring the country as Miss USA. On one particular occasion she spoke to a group of teenagers about the importance of keeping themselves morally clean and of resisting offers to use harmful substances. A national news magazine poked fun at her remarks and pointed out that in later competition for the Miss World title the "modestly dressed" Dianna had lost to a young woman from another country who was now posing unclad in pornographic magazines while sipping champagne. The implication was that Dianna's position was foolish and that real success was to be had in doing the opposite of what she had been telling the teenagers.

This ploy was simply a classic example of the tempter's technique of making that which is good seem bad and that which is bad appear good. Of this technique the scriptures say: "Woe unto them that call evil good, and good evil; that put darkness for light, and light for darkness; that put bitter for sweet, and sweet for bitter! . . . Which justify the wicked for reward, and take away the righteousness of the righteous." (Isaiah 5:20, 23.)

In spite of the efforts of the wayward, the wicked, and the worldly to put you down when you stand up for what is right, remember this admonition of the Prophet Joseph Smith: "It is our duty to concentrate all our influence to make popular that which is sound and good and unpopular that which is unsound" (*History of the Church* 5:286).

Be popular with the people who really count in the eternal scheme of things. Don't settle for the temporary, transitory, so-called popularity that pulls you down.

Elder Richard L. Evans offered the following insights: "You must realize that being popular is not simply 'going along with the gang.' It is not simply being handsome or a football star. Rather, popularity is a result of proper attitudes, conscious effort, and true leadership by maintaining high ideals." (*Improvement Era*, Mar. 1963, p. 215.)

8

The Art of Communication

The story is told of a driver whose car ran out of gas on a busy street. Fortunately, he was able to get the car off to the side of the road before it came to a complete stop. The man turned on his flasher signals, locked the car, and started off to find a gas station. He found one about four blocks away, purchased a can of gasoline, and returned to his car. After emptying the contents of the can into his tank he tried in vain to start his car.

Just then a helpful motorist pulled up behind him. The driver got out of his vehicle and approached the distressed man asking if he could do something for him. "Yes," replied the man. "My car won't start on its own, but if you could give me a push I believe I could get it to start." The second driver indicated he would be happy to help. "However," added the man in the stalled car, "my car has an automatic transmission and you will have to get up to about thirty miles per hour before my car will start." The second driver looked a bit puzzled, but nodding his head he returned to his car.

The first man fastened his safety belt, turned on his ignition key, put his car in gear and waited for the second man to line up the two bumpers and commence pushing. He was puzzled, however, to see the second man begin to back his car down the road where he finally came to a stop about thirty yards behind the first car. Suddenly, the second car lurched forward and the driver drove his car into the back bumper of the first car at a speed of thirty miles per hour. Repairing the damage cost several hundred dollars and the first man suffered a whiplash injury.

Now, obviously the first man did not mean that the driver of the second car had to be going the desired speed *before* he started to push the stalled car. What he meant to communicate was that *after* the two vehicles were lined up and the pushing had started, they would have to get up to about thirty miles per hour before the engine of the first car would turn over and run on its own power.

What went wrong in the communication between these two men? Weren't the words clear? Didn't they speak the same language? How often do people get into difficulty because they don't understand one another?

This story illustrates a problem of communication known as *bypassing.* Commonly understood words may be used by two individuals, but the intended meaning is lost and disaster often results from the miscommunication.

How often have your experienced a misunderstanding in communication, either as the sender or the receiver of a message? You have probably seen the humorous, yet so often true, statement: "I know you believe you understood what you think I said, but I am not sure you realize that what you heard is not what I said!"

Miscommunication and lack of communication are major problems in human relationships. A number of studies show that difficulties between parents and children, husbands and wives, employers and employees, students and teachers, and just plain people result from their inability to understand and be understood. "You just don't understand!" is a very common phrase.

This chapter will discuss some suggestions on how you can improve your ability to communicate more effectively. But first let's consider the meaning of communication and the ways in which you communicate.

True communication implies that there is a *sharing* of ideas and feelings; it is not a one-way effort. Effective communication requires both a sender and a receiver. I like the definition of communication given many years ago by a sociologist named Charles H. Cooley. He said communication is "the mechanism through which human relations exist and develop."

In what ways do you communicate? Whether you realize it or not, you are constantly sending out signals to others, even when your mouth is closed. Your clothing, posture, hair style, cosmetics, smile, hobbies, music, reading material, companions, and anything else that is identified with you, sends out messages. Just as the props used by a character in a movie or play help convey a message to the audience, in a similar fashion the things you surround yourself with convey messages to those who observe you. Are the signals you are sending to others through the use of your props the ones you want them to receive? Are your props appropriate to the character you want to be?

Even in verbal communication we sometimes send signals that may convey an unintended message on our part. Have you ever heard someone deny that he was angry but the tone of his voice and his flushed face made it plain that he really was angry? Voice inflections and intensity can considerably change the meaning of a spoken statement.

The use of words can often be misunderstood. For example, a nonmember who is invited by a Latter-day Saint to accompany him to the *stake* house may be disappointed to find himself in church instead of at a restaurant (steak house).

Let's discuss some of the things you can do to more effectively communicate with others.

Listen actively. Have you ever heard someone say, "Pay attention"? To *pay* means that you are giving something. Many problems in communication exist because people simply don't pay the price to understand the intended message. To pay attention implies that you are actively listening, that you are concentrating on what is being said. You don't allow your mind to wander but instead focus your attention on the message at hand. Effective listening is not a passive activity. It requires an effort on the part of the listener.

When you pay attention to another you convey a positive message that says, "You are worthwhile." To show disinterest is to send the opposite message.

Beware of duologues. A *dialogue* is an exchange of ideas between two parties where each is seeking to understand the other. A *duologue* (a word coined by

Professor Abraham Kaplan of the University of Michigan) is the expression of independent and unrelated thoughts between two parties where neither is listening to the other but each is concentrating solely on what he wants to say.

People who engage in duologues are like two television sets turned on to different channels, each sending a message but neither receiving what the other is sending. Sometimes games are played in which one gives the other person his *turn* and remains silent while he speaks. Maybe the silent one even nods his head occasionally or says "uh-huh" to show the other he is having his turn. But the silent one isn't really listening; he is only thinking about what he will say when it is his turn to speak. How often have you played this game? Someone once quipped that too often conversation is a game played where the first one to draw a breath is declared the listener.

Remember that perceptions differ. If you have ever listened to witnesses of the same event give different accounts of what happened you have seen the reality of differing perceptions. The way you see things may not necessarily be the way someone else views an event. Who is to say which is the correct version? Sometimes it is very difficult to declare that one version is more correct than another, even though they differ considerably.

A rather humorous story was told about a man and his wife, Mr. and Mrs. Rose, who were walking through town one night. Look at their experience as related in four different accounts to a man we'll call Craig.

Craig was walking down the street one afternoon when he ran into Mrs. Rose. "Hello there," he said, "I haven't seen you in quite some time. How have you been?" She responded by indicating she was well enough but that she wasn't quite sure about her husband's state of mind.

"What do you mean?" replied Craig.

"Well," continued Mrs. Rose, "the other night we were walking through town and I had on one of my nicest outfits. My cheeks were quite rosy from walking and I really think I looked quite attractive. Suddenly, a man stepped up and said something to me. I couldn't quite understand what it was, although I think he was complimenting me on my looks. Anyway, my jealous husband picked up a brick that happened to be lying close by on the sidewalk and banged the man on the head, leaving him lying on the ground."

After chatting for a few more minutes, Craig continued on down the street where he ran into Mr. Rose. "Well, hello, old friend," Craig called out. "I understand you've been breaking people's heads lately!"

"Oh," responded Mr. Rose, "you must have been talking with my wife. It was really fortunate that I saw that brick on the sidewalk. It gave me something to protect us with. There's no telling what might have happened if I had not acted so quickly."

"Do you really think that man intended to hurt you or rob you?" Craig asked.

"What else could have been his motive for sneaking up on us in the dark? I saw him sitting on the bus bench eying us," responded Mr. Rose. "It was a rather dark night, my wife had on her expensive jewelry, and I had a wallet full of cash. There is no question the man was up to no good."

Craig and Mr. Rose went their separate ways, and soon Craig saw a friend he had not seen for some time. "My word!" exclaimed Craig. "What happened to you? Have you been in an accident?" The friend had his head wrapped in bandages and both of his eyes were black-and-blue. He looked awful.

"Do you know if any lunatics have been on the loose lately?" responded his friend. "I was attacked by one just the other night."

He then related this account of his experience: "I was sitting on a bench in town waiting for the bus. I had been waiting for some time with no buses going by. I wasn't sure what time it was because I didn't have my watch with me. I saw this older couple walking and decided to ask them the time. I went up to them and in my most polite manner said, 'Pardon me, could you please tell me the time?' The man responded by picking something up and hitting me with it! The next thing I knew I was in the hospital with a cracked head."

Now, who is telling the correct story? The wife who thought her jealous husband wantonly attacked a would-be wolf? The husband who thought he was protecting himself and his wife from an attacker? Or the victim who simply wanted to know what time it was? Although you might be inclined to vote for the victim because his was the only *true* story in terms of the motive for the whole exchange, keep in mind that each was responding according to his or her perception of reality.

I mentioned that there were four accounts of this incident. The fourth account appeared in the newspaper. Under the headline "Man Found Unconscious" was the story of how the police had picked up an unconscious man who had obviously fallen to the ground in a state of drunken stupor and cracked his head on a loose brick. Now the public has yet another version of the story.

Do you see how facts can be confused with perception? Sometimes people are misunderstood because messages have become colored by individual perception. When you are having trouble communicating because someone disagrees with your version of an incident, sit down and talk it out without becoming defensive and thinking that your position is the only true one.

Try the feedback technique. Dr. Carl Rogers, a famous counselor, suggested the technique of feedback for helping people solve communication problems. If two people find themselves at an impasse in coming to an understanding of what each is trying to communicate, one says, "I will be quiet and listen to you explain your point of view. When you have finished explaining to me, I will then recount to you what I have heard you say. If I have misunderstood something, you will correct me. I will continue this process until I have related to your satisfaction what you have been trying to tell me. Then, when I am through, you will do the same for me."

This feedback approach may not bring agreement, because each individual may still hold to his originally held position, but it will bring understanding. At least each person will understand what the other is trying to communicate.

Some years ago I listened to a heated argument between two college students. Each was trying to convince the other of the correctness of his or her position. As the debate continued, I noticed that there really wasn't that much difference between the position each had taken but neither was understanding the other. Finally, in exasperation, the girl screamed at the fellow, "You're not listening to me!" With a startled look, he suddenly fell silent.

I joined in the conversation at this point and said, "That's right, Kim, Russ wasn't listening to you. But neither were you listening to him." I then suggested that if each would give the other a chance to present his or her point of view, without interruption, they might find some common ground for understanding. I was pleased to see them still talking in more subdued voices sometime later.

Look for common interests. If you find it difficult to talk with others, look for things you have in common that you can feel comfortable in talking about. Try talking about hobbies, sports, music, favorite things to do, goals and aspirations, current events, family, pets, books, food, scriptures, heroes, and the list could go on and on. Suppose you say there is nothing you have in common with another—what then?

I think the following story illustrates that if you try hard enough, you can find something in common with anyone. A former mission president, Elder Robert L. Backman, related the story as follows:

> One of the missionaries who served with me had a difficult time getting along with companions. I was required to transfer them frequently because they could not take it. Finally, I asked one of my finest missionaries to become his companion, urging him to do all he could to help his fellow missionary love his work. As I approached a conference in the city where they were laboring, I feared he, like his predecessors, would ask for a transfer. To my surprise, when I asked how he was getting along with his companion, he responded: "We are doing great! We discovered we had something in common. Neither of us has been to Africa!" (*Ensign*, Nov. 1987, p. 62.)

Be careful about dominating a conversation. Have you ever seen one of those wind-up mechanical mouths? You turn the key and watch the lips open and close in rapid fashion. Unfortunately, some people are like a mechanical mouth that never winds down. Somehow they have been stuck in the open position. They dominate the conversation and never allow anyone else to talk.

I am aware of people who become social outcasts, ostracized by others, because they don't know how to be quiet and listen. As some turn away, these mechanical mouths try even harder to be heard and succeed only in further alienating others. If you find people shying away from you, you may want to consider how much you dominate the conversation and start listening more to others.

Learn to listen to the language of silence. Although silence can serve as a weapon to destroy relationships, it can also serve a valuable purpose if effectively used. There are times when great messages can be communicated in silence.

A minister was once asked to take a tragic message to a mother and father who belonged to his congregation. Their son had been killed in an accident. Upon hearing the news, the heartbroken parents were unable to contain their grief and began to sob. Rather than trying to talk to them, the minister, with tears running down his cheeks, simply sat by them and held their hands. His empathic silence conveyed a greater message of love and support than any sermon or counsel may have done on that occasion.

I recall hearing the story of an old woman who was confined to a rest home and had not been heard to speak for about three years. Nothing that anyone had tried had broken through her wall of silence. She just sat in her rocking chair either staring into what seemed to be an empty space in front of her or with her head hanging down in sleep.

One day a new nurse was assigned to work with the silent woman. Nothing was expected of the nurse other than to take care of the routine duties of seeing to the woman's physical needs. However, this nurse was a sensitive, caring person who looked at her work as more than just a job. She saw her patients as human beings who needed to be loved as well as cared for. She pulled up a rocking chair alongside the woman and just rocked silently by her side for several hours every day, occasionally reaching over and gently touching the silent woman. After three days of this, the older woman turned to the new nurse and said, "You're so kind." The nurse had communicated loving empathy without a word being spoken and a miracle had occurred. The woman continued to improve under this new approach of caring communication.

Seek for the inspiration to know when to speak and when to be silent. Someone once said that people commit the same error with each other that they do in praying to God—they try to do all the talking and never take time to listen.

Look beyond the spoken word to the hidden agenda (the masked message). When effective meetings are conducted there is usually a written agenda that is followed. To a great extent people have agendas in their private conversations. Sometimes the items on these agendas are very evident, but occasionally they are hidden.

Just as silence speaks, sometimes the hidden agendas—the thoughts between or behind the spoken words—speak louder than what we actually may hear. Consciously or subconsciously—perhaps out of fear of rejection—we often mask the real message we intend to communicate.

What is the masked message in the following story?

A father was tucking his two young sons into bed one night. He kissed the younger one goodnight, but simply said "Good night" to four-year-old Adam.

As the father was leaving the room, he heard the soft whimpers of Adam. "What's the matter, son?" said the father. With tears running down his cheeks, the boy simply turned his face toward the wall and didn't answer.

"Adam, what's the trouble?" father persisted. After a minute of silence the youngster said, "I'm cold!" "Well, pull up your blanket," the father said in a somewhat annoyed voice. "Certainly you're big enough to do that."

Adam continued crying, perhaps even a little louder now, and the father in anger said, "Well, if you want to be stubborn you'll just have to be cold!" and he stalked angrily out of the room.

Adam cried himself to sleep.

Now, what was the problem here? Was Adam really cold? No! His father missed the masked message. Adam simply wanted to be reassured that he was loved just like his younger brother. "Daddy kissed him goodnight but not me," Adam said to himself. "Daddy must like my brother more than me."

Rather than becoming annoyed and angry at another, why not try to understand the reason behind what to you may seem strange behavior. Let others know you really care about them and that you want to understand them. Patience might be your greatest virtue in trying to understand masked messages. Let others know it is *safe* to convey their feelings to you.

Provide an atmosphere of safety. Honest, open communication thrives in an atmosphere of safety. People must feel that they can express thoughts and opinions in your presence without becoming the target of constant criticism or sarcasm. Don't be quick to judge. Leave that process to patient bishops and our loving Lord.

It is also important to allow another to complete the thought he wants to communicate without interrupting him. Don't be a dud who sits silently without expressing any thoughts of your own, but be cautious about wanting to jump too quickly into the conversation, cutting the other person off before he is finished.

Safeguard confidences. A deadly enemy of communication is the breaking of confidences. If others feel they cannot trust you with their messages, you will communicate at a very superficial level. Keep another's trust as sacred as if you had made a solemn covenant to do so.

Never betray a confidential conversation.

A discussion on how to more effectively communicate would be incomplete without saying something about spiritual communication. Elder Joseph B. Wirthlin has testified, "I know as never before that there is a form of communication that transcends the power of words." He indicated that while words are indispensable in our present form of communication "there is a great deal more to understanding than the use of mere words."

Elder Wirthlin also stated: "There is a mighty power that transcends the power of messages conveyed by words alone, and this is the power of messages communicated by the Spirit to our hearts. In every land and clime the sweet Spirit of our Savior communicates to all who seek the truth, regardless of tongues or dialect. It is a universal messenger to every heart in tune." (*Ensign*, Nov. 1975, p. 104.)

The universal language of the Spirit can communicate messages from unseen sources, even from the presence of God. I am not talking about foolish, false, and faddish things such as mysticism, wizardry, and the so-called new age harmonies. The language of the Spirit emanates from the presence of God. Satan seeks to deceive through his counterfeit methods. These should strictly be avoided. If you are righteous and prayerful, you can have the spirit of discernment to recognize the difference between the true peace of God's Spirit as opposed to the confusion created by the adversary.

Let me suggest some approaches to prayer that will assist you in your spiritual communications with your Father in Heaven:

Prepare. Place yourself in tune with the Spirit by approaching prayer in an unhurried fashion and in a location where you will not be disturbed. There is great meaning to the admonition, "When thou prayest, enter into thy closet [place of privacy], and when thou hast shut thy door, pray to thy Father who is in secret" (3 Nephi 13:6). Of course, this does not preclude praying constantly in your heart and at all times and in all places, as the scriptures admonish (see Alma 34:19–27; 3 Nephi 20:1).

Develop a personal relationship. Try to visualize your Father in Heaven in your mind. Talk to Him, not the inside of your hands or your pillow. Strive for the relationship described in the following statement: "There seemed to be a friendliness between my father and God, and when you heard him pray you would actually think the Lord was right there and that father was talking to him" (J. Golden Kimball in Thomas Cheney, *The Golden Legacy* [Salt Lake City: Peregrine Smith, Inc., 1976], pp. 15–16).

Plead with all your energy. Effective prayer is not a casual thing. You cannot communicate with God if you are in a hurry or if your mind is on other matters.

Several years ago a commercial company marketed a product called "Saint Spray," which was literally a canned prayer. Each container bore the picture of a saint and a printed prayer on the label. Customers were instructed to recite the prayer while spraying the scent around their homes. Contrast this superficial approach to prayer with Alma who "*labored* much in the spirit, *wrestling* with God in mighty prayer" (Alma 8:10; italics added).

President Ezra Taft Benson has given us this insight on prayer: "Each of us would become disturbed if a friend said the same few words to us each day, treated the conversation as a chore, and could hardly wait to finish it in order to turn on the TV and forget us" (*Ensign*, May 1977, p. 33).

Pause. Are you taking time to listen when you pray, or are your prayers a one-sided conversation? Elder Marvin J. Ashton has counseled, "Part of our worthwhile, urgency prayers today can be a reverent, quiet, listening period" (*Ensign*, May 1974, p. 37). Listen to the promptings that come to you, the thoughts that come to your mind, the burnings that come to your heart, or the peace that descends upon your soul. President Spencer W. Kimball cautioned, "Always expecting the spectacular, many will miss entirely the constant flow of revealed communication" (*Church News*, Jan. 5, 1974, p. C-2).

Proceed. When one arises from one's knees, prayer is not complete. President Ezra Taft Benson has counseled: "After making a request through prayer, we have a responsibility to assist in its being granted" (*Ensign,* May 1977, p. 33). Someone once said that we should pray as if everything depended upon the Lord and then get up and work as if everything depended upon us. Answers to prayers generally come in a cooperative effort between the person who prays and he who grants the petition.

One final thought about communicating through prayer. What if the things we request don't seem to be granted? Elder Neal A. Maxwell has offered us this helpful insight:

> Petitioning in prayer has taught me that the vault of heaven, with all its blessings, is to be opened only

by a combination lock: one tumbler falls when there is faith, a second when there is personal righteousness, and the third and final tumbler falls only when what is sought is (in God's judgment, not ours) 'right' for us. Sometimes we pound on the vault door for something we want very much in faith, in reasonable righteousness, and wonder why the door does not open. We would be very spoiled children if that vault door opened any more easily than it does now. I can tell, looking back, that God truly loves me by the petitions that, in his perfect wisdom and love, he has refused to grant me. Our rejected petitions tell us not only much about ourselves, but also much about our flawless Father." (*1976 Devotional Speeches of the Year* [Provo, Utah: Brigham Young University Press, 1977], p. 200.)

9

The Joy of Creative Dating

The dictionary says that a *paradox* is "something with seemingly contradictory qualities or phases." Dating is a paradox. The very thought of dating can elicit happy feelings and great expectations of fun and excitement, yet it can also cause emotional turmoil and considerable stress.

I knew of one young man who desperately wanted to go on dates, but every time he thought about asking a girl out he got sick to his stomach. I have known of numerous young people who are so excited about going out that they develop a rash, a cold sore, or break out in big pimples—usually on the end of their nose!

While on a date some young people are so anxious to have a successful experience that they don't act natural—they are not themselves. As a result, too often they say or do *dumb* things. Many dates have ended in tears of frustration and vows or fears of, "I'll never go on another date!"

Then there are those young people who want to date but never seem to have the opportunity. They wait patiently for the phone call that never comes. Some who have just turned sixteen, without an immediate invitation to date, seriously consider celibacy (remaining single all their lives).

Truly, dating is a paradox. It provides both agony and ecstasy.

In order to find joy in the dating years, there are some simple guidelines that should be considered.

First, understand the purpose of dating. In the early years of dating—generally through high school—dating is a social experience in which young people have the opportunity to develop social skills. It is an opportunity to get to know different individuals and to make new friends. You can discover attributes and traits in others that attract you and begin to fashion in your mind the ideals you want in a future marriage partner.

Be careful about becoming serious with another in your early teens. Avoid pairing off with one individual. Try to stick to group dating, where more than one couple is involved in the social activity. Have parties where no one person is another's date. Get to know a number of people and seek to make many friends. Avoid situations where high standards are not maintained.

An important guideline of dating, especially during the teen years, is to recognize the right and the obligation of parents to know and approve of your dating experiences.

Some years ago Elder Boyd K. Packer spoke of how foolish it would be to allow a total stranger to borrow an expensive family car without knowing who he was, where he was going to take the car, or when he was going to return it. Elder Packer pointed out that it is much more foolish for parents to allow their most precious possessions—their children—to be taken on dates by total strangers, without knowing where the two were going to go on their date or what time they expected to return home. (See Conference Report, Apr. 1965, pp. 69–71.)

Recognize that your parents' concern for your whereabouts is an expression of their love for you, not an indication of mistrust on their part.

Following high school, and particularly after the mission experience for the young men, dating takes on a new dimension. Although you should always consider a date as a prospective mate, and as a result be very careful about whom you date, as one matures in years the dating partners are particularly looked upon as potential marriage partners. Courtship becomes an important phase of dating at this point.

Another guideline to successful dating is to treat your date with respect. A date is a *person*, not a piece of property to be used for your personal pleasure.

Some years ago I read about a college fraternity that sponsored an "ugliest girl" party. Each of the members of the fraternity were to seek out a girl they considered to be ugly and invite her to the party. She was not to be told the true purpose of the party but upon arriving it would be very obvious to most of the girls that they were being used for the sick satisfaction of the boys involved.

Never, never should anyone seek amusement at the expense of another person's physical, spiritual, emotional, or psychological well-being. There is nothing "innocent" about this so-called kind of fun.

The Book of Mormon gives us this warning:

> And again I say unto you, is there one among you that doth make a *mock* of his brother, or that heapeth upon him persecutions?
>
> Wo unto such an one, for he is not prepared, and the time is at hand that he must repent or he cannot be saved! (Alma 5:30–31; italics added.)

On a truly fun-filled date no one gets hurt.

Seek wholesome activities, things that promote happy, guilt-free memories. This does not preclude a few so-called crazy activities. You can be *silly* without being *sinful*!

A group of young people decided to dress up like tourists, decked out with camera gear, and go around town pretending to take pictures of the local sights and citizens. They even asked people to pose with them so they could show the folks "back home" what people from this particular town looked like. There was no harm in their activity and there was no shame. It was simply silly—and a lot of fun.

If there is any question in your mind about the appropriateness of an activity or place, stay away! The discomfort you feel is the Spirit warning you to avoid something or someone. Surely sorrow will follow failure to heed spiritual promptings. Remember your divine heritage as children of an eternal King. When you go out on a date, be sure that you return with your crown untarnished.

An important guideline to joy in dating is to avoid getting serious too soon. Much opportunity for personal growth and developing friendships is lost if young people limit themselves to one steady partner during the high school years. Young women should be cautious of the recently returned missionary who wants to take you to visit the temple grounds on your first date.

Some years ago there was a popular song that contained the line, "Falling in love with love is grand." Unfortunately, there are some young people who focus all their attention on the *state* of love or the *state* of marriage and not on the prospective partner. Don't make the mistake of falling in love with love or with marriage. At the right time, fall in love with the proper *person*!

Speaking of avoiding getting too serious on dates, what do you do with the physically aggressive person? You know the kind—the octopus with arms all over you, the would-be backseat quarterback who is constantly making passes. (Just be sure the passes are "incomplete" or "intercepted.") Have you ever felt like you needed a referee to declare unauthorized "holding" penalties?

The counsel of Church leaders has always been to avoid peddling your affection in a cheap manner and to safeguard your virtue. In an area conference held in São Paulo, Brazil, President Spencer W. Kimball gave the following counsel to young people: "Keep your lives clean. Let there be no petting, no intimacies. Don't let anybody handle your body. That body is yours. It is given to you by your Heavenly Father. That body will be yours for millions of years. Even after you have died, you will be resurrected. Your body is destined to become a god or goddess. Only you can make it a god or goddess." (São Paulo Area Conference Report, Mar. 1, 1975, p. 42.)

How do you handle the issue of kissing? When should you kiss another and when should you resist another's attempt to kiss you? How much kissing is too much? Someone wisely observed that the kiss

Judas gave Jesus was one too many. Certainly, passionate kissing should be reserved for marriage, and the so-called "soul kiss" or "French kiss" is not something to be tampered with in casual dating. It can quickly excite emotions that become uncontrollable. President Kimball has given this important counsel:

> If the "soul kiss" with its passion were eliminated from dating there would be an immediate upswing in chastity and honor, with fewer illegitimate babies, fewer unwed mothers, fewer forced marriages, fewer unhappy people.
>
> With the absence of the "soul kiss" necking would be greatly reduced. The younger sister of petting, it should be totally eliminated. (Edward L. Kimball, ed. *The Teachings of Spencer W. Kimball* [Salt Lake City: Bookcraft, 1982], p. 28.)

One of the problems with casual kissing is that it seems to stimulate the desire for more rather than to satisfy a passing need. True, but tragic, words were coined by Shakespeare: "We have kiss'd away kingdoms and provinces" (*Antony and Cleopatra,* III.10.8).

"I know the dangers of kissing," someone says, "but how do I get out of a situation where I might be expected to participate in sharing physical affection when I don't want to?" Suppose a date asked you for a kiss or simply tried to kiss you without asking—what do you do? Humor has a way of relieving tension and people who use it appropriately can remain friends. It is a big help in tense or uncomfortable situations. Try using some of the following approaches:

- "Did you know that I am really a toad in disguise and if you try to kiss me you'll get warts on your lips?"

- "I'm sorry, but I have taken a vow never to kiss someone on the ____________ date." (Fill in the blank with the appropriate number.)
- "Did you know that I am taking karate lessons?"
- In response to the question, "Well, don't I deserve a little something for taking you on this date?" you can respond by reaching out and shaking his hand and saying, "Why, yes, thank you very much!" (If he is a returned missionary you might even add the word *Elder* to your thanks.)
- One of the most effective ways to deflate the mounting pressure to share affection is to keep a copy of the Book of Mormon in your purse or glove box and in response to an aggressive move simply say, "Mosiah 13:3!" Then open your scriptures to that passage and read the following to your startled suitor: "Touch me not, for God shall smite you if ye lay your hands upon me!"

If humor doesn't seem appropriate for the situation, consider the following straightforward ways of fending off a would-be kisser: "I'm sorry, but this is too soon for me to do that"; "I've made it my policy to take it slow when it comes to sharing physical affection"; or, simply use a most appropriate two-letter word—"No!"

Someone wrote these words which are worth remembering: "To let a fool kiss you is stupid, but to let a kiss fool you is worse." Reserve your affection for the right person and the right place. In the words of a prophet, "See that ye bridle all your passions, that ye may be filled with [true] love," not a fleeting and false imitation (Alma 38:12).

In recent years a creative custom has emerged in dating. No longer does it seem acceptable for a fellow to simply pick up the telephone and invite a young lady to go on a date. Nor does she simply give him an immediate yes or no answer.

For example, a young man who wants to invite a young lady to go on an ice skating or sleigh riding outing with him may invite her by writing his invitation on a piece of paper and freezing it in the middle of a huge ice block which he has delivered to her home. After the young lady has chipped through the ice to discover what the invitation is she is supposed to think of some clever way to give her answer. She might respond by sending him a gift certificate good for an ice cream cone at a friend's home, to which a note would be attached saying, "It would be cool and refreshing to go out with you. I'd love to."

Although this is a clever and novel way for young people to interact socially, there are some guidelines to consider in order to ensure that the experience is mutually enjoyable for both individuals involved.

As with anything, creative dating can be carried to an extreme. The quest to find some novel way to ask for, or respond to, a date can become so time consuming and expensive that the date itself is anticlimactic. When the fun goes out of the date and it almost becomes a burden for one or both individuals, it has lost one of its major purposes.

Another potential problem with creatively asking for a date is discourtesy on the part of the person being asked. The person who has done the asking should, of course, give plenty of lead time and not expect to put things together at the last minute. However, the person being asked needs to give a quick answer regardless of the amount of lead time. To keep the one who has done the asking hanging without a response is rude and insensitive. It is especially wrong to put off giving an answer with the hope that a supposed "better offer" may come from someone else. Be thoughtful, not thoughtless!

If there is a special occasion that warrants a truly creative approach, go for it! Give it your best shot. But use wisdom. You are trying to create a fun date, not win the creativity award for the year.

Dating should not become complicated. When you want to go out on a regular date, there is nothing wrong with just asking in person or on the telephone: "Hi, Hillary, this is Kris. I was wondering, if you are not busy next Friday night, would you like to go to a movie with me?"

By the way, notice in the above example that Kris did not say, "Hi, Hillary, this is Kris. *What are you doing Friday night?*" The problem with this approach is that Kris has asked for a commitment on Hillary's part without telling her what he has in mind. Suppose he wants to take her some place she wouldn't care to go, or suppose she says she is free and then he says, "Great! I have this cousin coming in from out of state and he needs a date for Friday night." Be considerate and be sure the person being asked understands the plans and the options so he or she does not feel forced into an awkward situation. If someone does ask you for a date without first explaining the conditions of the date, simply respond by saying: "What did you have in mind?"

One of the good things Kris did in calling Hillary on the phone is that he identified himself. Have you ever had the annoying experience of picking up the phone and having someone say, "Guess who this is?" One who uses this approach places the other person in a position where he might give the wrong answer and feel embarrassed. Don't force a person to play "twenty questions" with you. And, if you are on the receiving end of a phone call and the caller starts the conversation by asking, "Who is this?" respond by saying, "Who did you want to speak to?" or "Who were you calling?"

Let's return to the idea of creativity in dating. I have been alarmed at the amount of money some young people have spent on dates. For example, several young men told me that they had spent close to two hundred dollars on a date to a formal dinner and dance. That much money could buy a lot of college textbooks, help pay the rent, or be used to buy groceries in the mission field. A fun date need not be expensive, and it is not wise to spend great amounts of money in dating.

Consider the following ideas that cost very little and can be a lot of fun, especially if done in groups:

- Olympic games: Get a group together and re-create some track-and-field events such as the javelin toss using a long balloon; a discus throw using two paper plates taped together; races that include four people carrying another in a blanket or one blind-folded runner being coached by one who can see. Make up your own events and award homemade ribbons or medals.
- Creative creatures: From rocks, weeds, soap, silly putty, corn stalks—anything that can be carved, molded, painted, or glued together—create clever, funny little creatures, sculptures, or pieces of art.
- Put together an imaginary budget and go shopping to see what might be purchased. This is a good way to find out how much it might cost to live away from home or to get married.

- Take a walking tour of important historical sites in your area or just take a walk together.
- Go to the local airport, bus terminal, or train station and greet people who are arriving. A variation of this is to have one or two of your group carry empty suitcases and pretend they are leaving while the rest of you sadly bid them farewell.
- Board games: Play a trivia game, Monopoly, Life, or some other game that can be played in groups of four or more.
- Make up your own games: Use your imagination and create some games of your own. One such game is to select some words from the dictionary that most people would not be familiar with and write each down on a separate piece of paper along with its definition. Divide the group into two teams (more if you have a large group). Then take turns distributing to each member of a team pieces of paper from a hat or box. One of these papers has a word and the definition written on it and the rest just have the word. Those without the definition make up one of their own and the other team tries to guess who has given the correct definition.
- Put together a talent show for a local hospital or senior citizen's retirement home. Or, just go visit the patients or residents of these places and talk with them, read to them, or sing to or with them.
- Help cut out and color pictures for the Primary or the meetinghouse library.
- Go on a chore scavenger hunt: Give a list of small acts of service to teams that are sent out to accomplish chores and get a sign-off by the

people they have helped. Set a time limit and have treats waiting for the returning teams.

- Inspirational dates: Play charades by acting out scenes from the scriptures; review a Church book or recent article from a Church magazine; practice the missionary discussions; share inspirational experiences; research a gospel topic.
- Sports dates: Play volleyball, croquet, or create your own sports game such as playing golf using sticks, cans, and Nerf balls. Go on a bike ride, have a water fight, make and fly a kite. Play baseball using a stick and a Nerf ball or a piece of cloth that has been tied into a ball.
- Educational dates: Take a tour of the local library or a local business. Select topics and have everyone spend an hour in the library researching one; then share with the group what each has learned. Have a spelling contest or a "name a famous person" contest.

The list of creative, inexpensive, and fun things to do is endless if you will just use a little imagination. Strive for dating experiences that allow you to get to know others and to develop social skills and friendships in wholesome ways. Going to a movie or watching a video allows for very little interaction, and the contents might even be harmful.

One of the nice things about most of the foregoing suggestions for creative dating is that these things can be done in groups. You don't need to pair off as couples to enjoy many social activities. If you are not dating, get your friends together and create some fun group activities.

Remember, dating should be fun. With the right attitude, high standards of conduct, and a little imagination you can create some great experiences!

10

Youth as Leaders

"I don't need to read this chapter. I'm not a leader!"

Wrong! Think again. This chapter is for *all* youth.

It doesn't matter whether you have been officially called as a leader in your school, church unit, social group, or club. You have been sent to earth at this particular time to be a leader, an example and a model of righteousness for others, and a "light unto the world" (D&C 103:9; see also 115:5).

Elder Vaughn J. Featherstone has said: "What you do now, today, may have far-reaching consequences. I believe today's Aaronic Priesthood and young women of the Church will lead the youth of the world through the most trying time in history." (*Ensign,* Nov. 1987, p. 29.)

You were sent to earth to be a leader of righteousness regardless of any other calls that may come to you. A true leader stands up for what is right. The young man or young woman who uses clean language, who holds high moral standards, who avoids cheating, lying, or stealing, who is courteous and considerate of others—such a person is a leader in the highest sense of the word.

A true leader leaves no question in others' minds where he stands on issues of right and wrong. He inspires confidence, and others are usually willing to follow his example. Occasionally, however, a leader may have to plod a path alone because of others' unwillingness to follow a proper example. When prophets such as Elijah or Ether found themselves alone because of their people's rebellion, they did not cease to be the leaders God had designated them to be (see 1 Kings 18; Ether 13:13).

To be true to principles is to be a leader. To buckle under pressure, joining the crowds in a wrong course of action, is to cease to be a leader.

A leader should lift and inspire others to greater heights of accomplishment and to the highest standards of conduct. President Harold B. Lee gave the following wise counsel: "You cannot lift another soul until you are standing on higher ground than he is. You must be sure, if you would rescue the man, that you yourself are setting the example of what you would have him be. You cannot light a fire in another soul unless it is burning in your own soul." (*Ensign,* July 1973, p. 123.)

Elder J. Richard Clarke told the following story of a young man whose actions helped lift others:

> One of our greatest needs is for true witnesses among our youth. Young people need models from their own generation. Thankfully we have a tremen-

dous army of latter-day sons and daughters of Helaman, stripling "Saturday's warriors," who are not ashamed of the gospel of Jesus Christ. Rather, they have turned this commitment to the Lord into an advantage. Let me tell you of one.

Steve Hawes is the student body president at New Canaan High School in Connecticut. Of its twenty-three hundred students, only twenty-four are Latter-day Saints. Steve ran unopposed in a landslide election. This is impressive. But even more impressive is Steve's moral courage—his commitment to living the principles of the gospel.

The Hawes family lived for a time in Tampa, Florida. Steve played junior high football and basketball. When his family was preparing to move to Connecticut, the coach told Steve's father how much he appreciated and admired Steve, not just because he is a fine athlete, but because of his deep religious convictions.

"He doesn't preach sermons; he just quietly lives his religion each day. I remember," said the coach, "a group of us were in the squad room, and one of the boys pulled out a copy of *Playboy* magazine. They opened to the centerfold and began to make some vulgar comments.

"I noticed Steve walk away, so I followed him and asked if anything was wrong. He said, 'I'm okay, Coach, but that just isn't my kind of thing.' "

The coach said, "Steve made us all better people. When he joined us, most of the guys were swearing. Then they stopped swearing around Steve, and after a while, they pretty well stopped swearing altogether."

When I heard this tribute, I thought of Paul's counsel to Timothy: "Be thou an example of the believers, in word, in conversation, in charity, in spirit, in faith, in purity" (1 Tim. 4:12). (*Ensign*, May 1985, p. 75.)

A leader is courteous to those with whom he works. He treats them with respect and consideration.

I remember reading of an incident involving General Dwight David Eisenhower that occurred during World War II. He was coming down a stairway one day when a young soldier, hurrying up the stairs to accomplish some task, ran into the five-star general and knocked him off his feet.

Suppose this had happened to you? If you were the soldier, what reaction might you have expected from the leader you had just knocked to the floor? If you were the general, how would you have responded?

Now, General Eisenhower might have given the lowly soldier a real dressing down or he might have immediately had him transferred to some forsaken military outpost. The young trooper was astonished, however, when the general said: "Wouldn't you think that an old man would wear his glasses so that he could see where he was going?"

What an act of courtesy, compassion, and charity!

When you have been knocked off your feet—physically, verbally, socially, psychologically—don't be too quick to take reprisals. Try a little kindness and see if it won't soften another's feelings as well as your own. Don't be too quick to put another person down. Use your authority wisely.

The Doctrine and Covenants provides this warning and counsel:

> We have learned by sad experience that it is the nature and disposition of almost all men, as soon as they get a little authority, as they suppose, they will immediately begin to exercise unrighteous dominion. . . .
>
> No power or influence can or ought to be maintained by virtue of the priesthood [or leadership position], only by persuasion, by long-suffering, by gentleness and meekness, and by love unfeigned.

> By kindness, and pure knowledge, which shall greatly enlarge the soul without hypocrisy, and without guile—
>
> Reproving betimes with sharpness when moved upon by the Holy Ghost; and then showing forth afterwards an increase of love toward him whom thou hast reproved, lest he esteem thee to be his enemy. (D&C 121:39–43.)

If you find yourself chewing someone out or reprimanding them in anger, with a raised voice and flushed face, it is *not* the Holy Ghost who has moved you. Any deserved reproving should be done calmly and in the spirit of kindness and helpfulness. A leader does not overlook mistakes. He does, however, work in a kindly manner to correct them.

A leader is willing to work. He does not sit idly by asking others to shoulder the burdens. He does his share and then some. There should never be any question in the minds of others as to a leader's willingness to help in the assigned task.

Elder James E. Faust has given us the following counsel: "The most encompassing short course on leadership was given by the Savior himself: 'And he saith unto them, Follow me' (Matthew 4:19). A leader cannot ask of others what he is not willing to do himself. Our safest course is to follow the example of the Savior, and our security is to listen to and follow the direction of his prophet, the President of the Church." (*Ensign*, Nov. 1980, p. 35.)

An important aspect of leadership is learning how to be a good follower. One must know how to *take* directions if he is ever going to effectively *give* directions. Even Jesus Christ followed the directions of his divine Father: "I came into the world to do the will of my Father," the Savior said (3 Nephi 27:13). Remember his classic statement of humble submissiveness in the Garden of Gethsemane? "Father, if thou be willing, remove this cup from me: nevertheless not my will, but thine, be done" (Luke 22:42).

Yet another important part of leadership is being prepared. None of us knows when a call to serve in an official assignment may come. If you familiarize yourself with principles of leadership prior to such a call, you can more quickly, and more effectively, fulfill your calling. Until such calls come, however, don't waste your time waiting. Look for ways to be of service to others now, for service is what leadership is all about.

The life of King Benjamin is an excellent illustration of one who knew that leadership meant service. In reporting on his ministry, he counseled his people to follow his example: "Behold, ye have called me your king; and if I, whom ye call your king, do labor to serve you, then ought not ye to labor to serve one another?" (Mosiah 2:18.)

Some years ago a customer wrote to the chairman of the board of a very successful store in a large city. The customer indicated that he was disturbed because "a very nice-looking woman" was frequently seen picking dead leaves from plants in the store. "Surely," the customer said, "you can find a better position for a person of such obvious quality."

The chairman wrote to the customer to thank him for his letter and his concerns. However, explained the store's leader, "the only higher position the woman in question could have would be my job. You see she is a member of our board of directors and insists on getting directly involved in making the store as attractive as possible."

A leader is concerned about his area of responsibility and is willing to do whatever is necessary and appropriate to make it successful. A leader does not interfere with another's delegated responsibility, but if he sees something that needs to be done, he is not afraid to roll up his sleeves and help.

The president of a company that manufactured pet food once called a press conference to introduce a new line of dog food. After he had extolled the virtues of the vitamins contained in the new product and its irresistible taste to dogs, a hungry animal was brought on stage to demonstrate the truth of the president's claims. Unfortunately, the dog was unnerved by the cameras and strange people present. After sniffing the plate of dog food, the animal backed off and refused to eat it.

Suppose you were in the president's shoes. What would you have done to save the moment?

Sensing that an explanation of the dog's behavior would not suffice, the president acted without delay. He picked up the plate and said, "Well, I guess Bowser is not in the mood to eat right now, but let me tell you that this dog food is so good that even people could eat it." With that, he commenced eating.

To be an effective leader, one must be able to react positively and quickly, particularly in a moment of great challenge.

A leader must be prepared for the unforeseen. A leader must inspire confidence in what he says and does so that others will follow.

I heard of a tombstone that read: "Come, Follow Me!" Someone with a sense of humor, but also with a desire to follow the right kind of leaders, etched the following below the original statement: "To follow you, I'm not content; Until I know, which way you went!"

Leadership is a trust. Others place confidence in a leader and trust that he or she will lead them correctly. The dictionary defines trust as "assured reliance on the character, ability, strength, or truth of someone or something." I recall hearing President David O. McKay once say, "To be trusted is greater than to be loved."

A leader must live worthy of others' trust. A true leader will not give his followers cause for concern about his trustworthiness. This means that he should make decisions based on what is best for the individuals he leads, never based on what is convenient or self-serving to the leader himself.

If you are serving as a leader in any organization, there are those who have placed their trust in you. Even if you are not currently serving in an officially called position of leadership, remember that God has sent you here on earth at this particular time of history to be a leader and a light for good.

Trust is an attribute of God. Perhaps one of the reasons why God is God is that He can be fully trusted. He never asks anything of us that will not be for our best good, and He never makes a promise that will not be kept. He is the great prototype of trust.

A good leader will follow this example and only ask his followers to do things that will be for their best good. He will never make unreasonable and unrighteous demands.

There is an interesting story that illustrates this principle in the book *The Little Prince.* The prince requested that the powerful king command that a sunset occur for his pleasure. The king explains the unreasonable nature of such a request as follows:

> "If I ordered a general to fly from one flower to another like a butterfly, or to write a tragic drama, or to change himself into a sea bird, and if the general did not carry out the order that he had received, which one of us would be in the wrong?" the king demanded. "The general, or myself?"

> "You," said the little prince firmly.
>
> "Exactly. *One must require from each one the duty which each one can perform,*" the king went on. *"Accepted authority rests first of all on reason.* If you ordered your people to go and throw themselves into the sea, they would rise up in revolution. *I have the right to require obedience because my orders are reasonable.*" (Antoine De Saint Exupery, *The Little Prince* [New York: Harcourt, Brace & World, Inc., 1971], p. 45; italics added.)

Do you get the picture? A leader must make reasonable requests of those he wants to follow him.

Occasionally trusts are violated. Judas is a classic example of one called to a high position of trust and leadership who turned traitor to his trust. Employees who cheat their employers, missionaries who violate mission rules, children who deliberately break solemn promises to parents, anyone who goes back on his word—these all break a trust and to that extent become traitors. The actions of traitors always bring suffering and sorrow, often to innocent bystanders and loved ones.

The world lives after the manner of the master deceiver, the devil. He lies and cheats to take advantage of others' weaknesses. A classic example of this kind of leader is found in the Book of Mormon. The wicked Amalickiah led many people astray and caused much suffering because of his false flatteries, deceitful lies, and downright treachery. In referring to the results of Amalickiah's evil leadership, Alma wrote: "Yea, and we also see the great wickedness one very wicked man can cause to take place among the children of men" (Alma 46:9).

A true leader stands for correct principles regardless of the pressure brought upon him to bend. The first president of Brigham Young University, Karl G.

Maeser, was this kind of a leader. His high code of honor could not be broken by pressure. It is reported that he once drew a circle around himself and said, "If I gave my word that I would stand in that circle and not move until told to do so by proper authority, I would die before I would step outside that circle of honor." Such should be the stance of a true leader.

If you have accepted an assignment, your honor requires that you do your best to fulfill your responsibility. The prophet Elijah posed an important question when he said, "How long halt ye between two opinions?" (1 Kings 18:21.) When you know what is right—do it!

The Lord said to early leaders of the Church, "Attend to thy calling and thou shalt have wherewith to magnify thine office" (D&C 24:9). To "attend to" something means to pay attention to it or to give time for it. To "magnify" an office means to enlarge upon it in a positive way. Do not confuse magnifying an *office* with enlarging one's *head.*

Whatever your leadership responsibility may be, no matter how menial or mundane you may consider it, give it your best. The Lord has promised to bless those who seek to serve with all their might. Above all, don't waste your time wishing for some other assignment. Alma gave wise counsel when he said, "Why should I desire more than to perform the work to which I have been called?" (Alma 29:6.)

Don't worry about credits and bylines. If your name is not printed in bold letters on the program or in bright lights on billboards, what does it matter? When Jesus performed services in behalf of others, he sought anonymity. "Go and tell no man," was His frequent counsel to those He had helped. When He volunteered to be our Savior, He said to the Father, "The glory be thine forever" (Moses 4:2). Concern yourself with serving the very best you know how in the assignment you have, not with accolades and applause.

A young boy had his heart set upon participating in his school play. He talked about the various important parts that he might be asked to play. On the day the selections were to be made he went off to school full of enthusiasm and great expectations. His mother anxiously waited for him to return after school that night. She worried that he might be deeply disappointed if he were not chosen for one of the roles in the play. As she looked out of the window, she finally saw her young son approaching. She was relieved to see the gleeful gait with which he walked and the smile upon his face. He rushed into the house and threw his arms around her saying: "Mother, guess what? I've been chosen to clap and cheer."

Sometimes we need to step aside and "clap and cheer" for those occupying center stage. It doesn't make us any less important. Plays could not be successful with just the "stars." Supporting casts, stage hands, directors, and audiences are all important. Whatever you are called upon to do, consider adopting the attitude of one who said: "But I do not joy in my own success alone, but my joy is more full because of the success of my brethren" (Alma 29:14).

Effective leadership requires total commitment. A chicken was once overheard to say that she didn't mind making a contribution to a breakfast of bacon and eggs. However, a hog rejoined, "Sure, that's easy for you to say. You only have to make a *contribution*. For me it is a *total commitment!*"

Alma was a committed leader. On one occasion he had fulfilled a tough assignment to teach the people in the city of Ammonihah. They were rebellious and rude. In spite of his best efforts they "withstood all his words, and reviled him, and spit upon him, and caused that he should be cast out of their city" (Alma 8:13). However, while he was journeying to his next assignment an angel of the Lord instructed him to return to Ammonihah to preach to the people. Take note of Alma's response to this request: "And it came to pass that after Alma had received his message from the angel of the Lord *he returned speedily* to the land of Ammonihah" (Alma 8:18; italics added).

Alma might have felt justified in refusing to return to Ammonihah. He might have said, "Well, I've already done my best. Why should I have to go back? Let somebody else try!" But he didn't. In spite of the toughness of his assignment and the personal abuse he had taken in trying to fulfill his assignment, Alma "returned speedily." A good leader will serve in spite of personal inconvenience and will go beyond the minimum that his assignment requires.

To be successful as a leader one must be prayerful and listen to the promptings of the Spirit. To rely solely upon one's own talents, without seeking the Lord's help, is to court failure. The words of the young prophet Samuel should be on the lips of every leader: "Speak, Lord; for thy servant heareth" (1 Samuel 3:9–10).

The Lord rarely speaks with an audible voice; therefore, you must cultivate a sensitivity to those warm whispers that come to the soul—the peaceful yet powerful thoughts that come into the mind, the burnings that come into the bosom.

President Harold B. Lee counseled:

> The most important thing you can do is to learn to talk to God. Talk to Him as you would talk to your father, for He is your Father, and He wants you to talk to Him. He wants you to cultivate ears to listen, when He gives you the impressions of the Spirit to tell you what to do. If you learn to give heed

> to the sudden ideas which come to your minds, you will find those things coming through in the very hour of your need. If you will cultivate an ear to hear these promptings, you will have learned to walk by the Spirit of revelation. (*Church News*, Mar. 3, 1973, p. 3.)

A few years ago I had the privilege of sitting in on an interview being conducted by Elder Loren C. Dunn, of the First Quorum of the Seventy, as he counseled a woman being called to serve on a Church writing committee. He gave her some wise and powerful counsel. He said, "It is not difficult to find writers. It is difficult to find one who can convey spirituality and build testimony. Write by the Spirit and others will receive by the Spirit. Writing is secondary; building testimony is primary!"

Elder Dunn then gave this very significant counsel: "With every calling there is a mantle and a spirit that is unique. You could use your talents and never apply the mantle!"

Make the Lord your full partner in everything you do. Rely upon the Spirit for help.

If you are to lead effectively you must do so by the Spirit. Use the mantle that has been given to you. Recognize your right to receive revelation for your assignment and live worthy to be in tune with the promptings of the Spirit.

Youthful leaders should keep in mind the counsel of the Apostle Paul to his young friend and companion, Timothy: "Let no man despise [look down upon] thy youth; but be thou an example of the believers, in word, in conversation, in charity, in spirit, in faith, in purity" (1 Timothy 4:12).

When you fail to set the proper example, you set up stumbling blocks for others. Alma reminded his wayward son Corianton that when the Zoramites saw his bad conduct they refused to believe the message he was sent to bring to them (see Alma 39:11). Years earlier Alma had also observed that "the wickedness of the [members of the] church was a great stumbling-block to those who did not belong to the church; and thus the church began to fail in its progress" (Alma 4:10).

It does not matter whether a member of Christ's Church has been called to serve in an officially designated leadership assignment. By virtue of his membership in the Church, each is a leader with a responsibility to share the gospel message with others. Being a good example is critically important to fulfilling that sacred assignment.

No matter what your current status of leadership, take to heart the following counsel by one of the Lord's Apostles, Elder Howard W. Hunter:

> May I say once more to the youth of the Church— prepare, believe, be ready, have faith. Do not say or do or be that which would limit your service or render you ineffective in the kingdom of God. Be ready when your call comes, for surely it will come. Keep your gospel shoes on, or as Paul wrote to the Ephesians, "Stand therefore, having . . . your feet shod with the preparation of the gospel of peace." (Ephesians 6:14–15.) (*Ensign*, May 1978, p. 35.)

The Relationship That Matters Most

III

11

Come Unto Christ

All that we have talked about in this book matter very little if you do not seek for the one thing that really counts. The way you will achieve your divine destiny, effectively deal with peer pressure, make correct choices, feel good about yourself, develop characteristics that will help you develop friendships and communicate more effectively is to do what the ancient prophet Moroni suggested and "come unto Christ."

> Nothing that is good denieth the Christ, but acknowledgeth that he is.
>
> And *ye may know that he is, by the power of the Holy Ghost*; wherefore I would exhort you that ye deny not the power of God; for he worketh by power, according to the faith of the children of men, the same today and tomorrow, and forever. . . .

> And Christ truly said unto our fathers: If ye have faith ye can do all things which are expedient unto me. . . .
>
> And again I would exhort you that ye would *come unto Christ,* and lay hold upon every good gift, and touch not the evil gift, nor the unclean thing. . . .
>
> Yea, *come unto Christ,* and be perfected in him, and deny yourselves of all ungodliness; and if ye shall deny yourselves of all ungodliness, and love God with all your might, mind and strength, then is his grace sufficient for you, that by his grace ye may be perfect in Christ; and if by the grace of God ye are perfect in Christ, ye can in nowise deny the power of God. (Moroni 10:6–7, 23, 30, 32; italics added.)

Do you know why it is important to "come unto Christ"? Do you know what he has done for you? Do you realize where you would be without his gifts of grace and love? Do you recognize that Christ is the means whereby we come to our Heavenly Father?

Centuries before you and I came to this earth as helpless infants to be nurtured by loving parents, friends, and family, we were born as spirit children into the household of God. We were loved by heavenly parents and were taught of the divine destiny available to each of us. Our eldest brother, the firstborn in the spirit world, was especially kind and good, and there is no doubt we learned much from Him.

Finally, Father brought us together in a council and presented a plan for our further progression. I imagine that the proceedings of that council went similar to what I've described in the following paragraphs.

We were told that if we were to become all that we were capable of becoming, we would need to leave our heavenly home. We would be sent to earth to receive a physical body. We would also gain experiences in mortality that were not available in the spirit world. We would be tested to see if we would do all things that God required of us and to see if we would stand firm in the face of adversity and temptations of the flesh. The stakes were high! If we failed we would forever forfeit the right to return to our heavenly home. If we succeeded we were promised a fulness of all that God Himself possessed. Nothing would be held back.

I suppose we were excited in anticipating this new adventure, as well as concerned about our abilities to succeed. I'm sure we also experienced a sense of homesickness in knowing that we would be leaving our heavenly parents for a time. Yet, if we were to fulfill our divine potential, there could be no other way.

Father explained that one of our noble brothers and one of our saintly sisters would be selected to receive the first physical bodies and become the first man and woman on the earth. He said that they would be placed on the earth in a state of innocence. But in order to experience the necessary opposition in life and to provide earthly bodies for the hosts of heaven destined to inhabit this new home, our first earthly parents would have to make a difficult choice. If they chose correctly they would be banished from the luxury and leisure of Eden and sent into the harsh realities of an often cruel and lonely world.

This exile, with all its consequences, was called the Fall. From this point on, Adam and Eve, our first earthly parents, and all their posterity would be subject to pain, disease, sorrow, and adversity in every form. On the other hand, they would have opportunities for happiness and experiences that would not otherwise have been possible, including conceiving and rearing children.

Father explained that the Fall would bring about two deaths: a spiritual death, which was being cast out of His presence; and a physical death, the separation of the spirit from the body. In order to be redeemed from these two deaths, Father's plan required the great sacrifice on the part of One who would become the Savior of us all. Two stepped forward to offer themselves for this important assignment.

The first to step forward was Father's firstborn in the spirit world, our eldest brother. He was so much like Father in appearance and in actions. He spoke with great power and undoubtedly expressed his great love for all of his brothers and sisters in the spirit world. His simple offer to serve as our Savior was a classic example of obedience: "Father, *thy* will be done, and the glory be *thine* forever" (Moses 4:2; italics added).

The second offer came from one who possessed great leadership abilities but who was afflicted with a fatal case of selfishness and pride. He was known as Lucifer. He sought personal glory and offered an amendment to Father's plan. He proposed to save all mankind by forcing them to conform to prescribed laws. There would be no choice in the matter. But, he said, because he would do this great thing he wanted to exalt himself above our Father and become the God whom we would worship. His plan was totally self-serving. He really didn't care about saving us. He simply wanted power and glory for himself.

There really was no question about who should be selected. Father knew that the amended plan would destroy the agency of man and create eternal misery for each of us. Under such a plan we would never reach our divine potential. Lucifer's insidious offer was rejected and the firstborn was chosen as the Savior who would come to earth as the Babe of Bethlehem, with power to redeem us from the effects of the Fall.

Insanely jealous of Jesus and angry with God and those of us who failed to support his bid for power, Lucifer and his followers openly rebelled. "He became Satan, yea, even the devil, the father of all lies, to deceive and to blind men, and to lead them captive at his will, even as many as would not hearken unto [God's] voice" (Moses 4:4). Having forfeited his chances for happiness and joy, he became "miserable forever," and he now seeks "that all men might be miserable like unto himself" (2 Nephi 2:18, 27).

Consider the consequences of the choices you make. When you choose to do wrong, to go against what you know or feel to be right, you choose to follow the one who seeks your misery. On the other hand, when you make correct choices, following your conscience—the Light of Christ—and the promptings of the Holy Ghost, you choose the joy that comes with following Christ.

The choice between misery and happiness is simply a continuation of the choices available to us when our Father in Heaven presented his plan in our preearthly home. To come unto Christ is to follow "the great plan of happiness" (Alma 42:8).

Do you know how Christ redeemed us from the effects of the Fall and made eternal joy and happiness available to those who would be obedient to our Father in Heaven's will? Let us consider the two major consequences of the Fall previously mentioned: spiritual death—being cast out of God's presence—which comes as a result of our sinning; and physical death—the separation of body and spirit—which will come to all mankind as a natural consequence of living.

While all of us are sons and daughters of God, being born of heavenly parents in the spirit world, only Jesus Christ, the firstborn in the spirit world, had God as the father of his earthly body. Thus, He is known as the Only Begotten in the flesh. He is literally the Son of God.

The mother of Jesus was a very special mortal woman named Mary. She undoubtedly was a model of spirituality, purity, and every virtue of womanhood in order to be worthy of her role.

Jesus inherited power over death from His divine Father. If He chose to, He never would have to die. However, from His mortal mother He inherited the capacity to die. His mixed parentage of an immortal Father and a mortal mother gave Him this choice. By allowing His life to be taken on the cross at Calvary, Jesus was able to exercise the power that brought forth His body from the confines of the tomb that first Easter morning. This same power will ultimately bring the resurrection to each of us. Truly we sing with great joy: "Let the whole wide earth rejoice. Death is conquered, man is free. Christ has won the victory." (*Hymns*, no. 199.)

The gift of the resurrection is a gift of grace. There is absolutely nothing that any mortal being needs to do to merit this free gift other than to be born and to die. Of all our Father in Heaven's children, only Satan and the evil spirits who joined in his rebellion against God will be denied physical birth, death, and resurrection.

There is another gift which Christ offers to us which requires something from us. In order to overcome the effects of the spiritual death—being cast out of God's presence—a great sacrifice of One who was sinless had to be made. This sacrifice is little understood by the world in general. Most Christians focus their attention on the cross and the gruesome events of Golgotha and seem totally unaware of the significance of the Garden of Gethsemane.

A single verse in the Bible alludes to this great sacrifice: "And being in an agony he prayed more earnestly: and his sweat was as it were great drops of blood falling down to the ground" (Luke 22:44).

Fortunately we have additional scripture which explains what occurred on that sacred yet terrible occasion. An ancient American prophet said that Christ's bleeding from every pore came because of "his anguish for the wickedness and the abominations of his people" (Mosiah 3:7).

Jesus Christ voluntarily took upon himself the suffering brought about by every single sin that was ever committed or will be committed by every individual who has or will inhabit this earth. He also suffered in behalf of countless people who inhabit the other worlds He has created. In addition, He suffered for "all of our sickness and grief and pain of every kind." (See *Ensign*, May 1988, pp. 16–17, 69; 2 Nephi 9:21.)

Think of all the pain you have personally experienced, combine that with the total pain and sorrow suffered by the billions of people who have inhabited this earth or yet will, and you still don't have any true measure of the price paid by Christ in Gethsemane. His suffering was so great that He said it caused Him, who is "God, the greatest of all, to tremble because of pain, and to bleed at every pore, and to suffer both body and spirit" (D&C 19:18).

Unlike the gift of resurrection, this gift of God—the suffering of the Savior for our sins—is not without a price to be paid on our part. In order to put this gift in force in our lives, we must repent from the sins we have committed (see 2 Nephi 2:7; Alma 34:16). If we fail to do so, the gift of Gethsemane loses its force for us personally and we must pay our own price (see D&C 19:16–17). This is like saying to the Savior, "I don't care about your suffering for me. I reject your offer of grace in my behalf." In this case a double price will be paid: the one already paid by the sinless Son of God and the one to be paid by the unrepentant sinner.

Do you see why it is so important to "come unto Christ"? He loves you and is looking out for your welfare. To choose to be disobedient, slothful, and unrepentant is to reject Christ's offer of love and to follow after the wretched creature who seeks your misery. To "come unto Christ" is to choose eternal joy and progression. To choose otherwise is to select spiritual death, sorrow, and damnation—which means an end to your progression.

The combination of Christ's two gifts to us is called the Atonement. Through His atoning sacrifices, our Savior overcame the effects of the Fall. Through his grace we will be resurrected; through our obedience and repentance, combined with Christ's grace, we shall return to God's presence.

"If Christ overcame the effects of the Fall, why then," some ask, "is man referred to as 'carnal, sensual, and devilish,' with a natural inclination towards evil (see Alma 42:10; Ether 3:2)? If my nature is to make wrong choices, what chance do I really have to be good?"

The problem does not come with your nature, but with a misunderstanding of what the scriptures and the prophets have said regarding what is known as the natural or fallen man. For example, when considering the words of the brother of Jared that "because of the fall our natures have become evil continually" (Ether 3:2), you have to look at the context of his statement. At the time he spoke these words he was approaching God on a matter that he felt might anger the Lord. In the context of speaking of his *own* feelings of unworthiness he generalized to *all* mankind. From the days of the Fall, man has become "evil continually" *only* when he has continually *chosen* evil, not because of an inherent flaw in his nature.

I cannot stress strongly enough the message of this book's first chapter, "Your Divine Potential." You are a child of God and inherently have seeds of goodness planted deep within your soul. When you make improper choices, you go against your *true* nature.

Statements regarding the evil nature of man must be looked at in light of other scriptures and statements by prophets. For example, note these words of the Nephite prophet-king Benjamin: "For the natural man is an enemy to God, and has been from the fall of Adam, and will be, forever and ever, *unless he yields to the enticings of the Holy Spirit,* and putteth off the natural man and becometh a saint through the atonement of Christ" (Mosiah 3:19; italics added).

President Spencer W. Kimball said that "the 'natural man' is the 'earthy man' who has allowed rude animal passions to overshadow his spiritual inclinations" (*Ensign,* Nov. 1974, p. 112).

Alma taught his wayward son that when men are in a carnal state (meaning they overemphasize pleasures of the flesh as opposed to focusing on the things of the Spirit), they "have gone contrary to the nature of God" and "are in a state contrary to the nature of happiness" (Alma 41:11).

Elder Marion G. Romney gave us the following insights regarding our nature:

> I know the scriptures say that "the natural man is an enemy to God." . . . And so he is when he rejects the promptings of the Spirit and follows the lusts of the flesh. But he is not an enemy to God when he follows the promptings of the Spirit.
>
> I firmly believe that notwithstanding the fact that men, as an incident to mortality, are cast out from the

> presence of God and deprived of past memories, *there still persists in the spirit of every human soul a residium from his pre-existent spiritual life which instinctively responds to the voice of the Spirit of Christ* until and unless inhibited by the free agency of the individual." (*Improvement Era,* June 1964, p. 506; italics added.)

Each of us is born with the Light of Christ. We have the power to know good from evil (see Moroni 7:16; Helaman 14:31). The choice is ours. Furthermore, those who have been baptized and have received the gift of the Holy Ghost through the laying on of hands have additional help, for this member of the Godhead "will show unto you all things what ye should do" (2 Nephi 32:5).

The only way that Satan gets power over us is if we give it to him (Mosiah 16:2–5). Righteousness on our part restricts his power (1 Nephi 22:26). A man who served as a General Authority for twenty-four years, Elder ElRay L. Christiansen, said: "In all his evil doings, the adversary can go no further than the transgressor permits him to go; . . . and when the Holy Ghost is really within us, Satan must remain without" (Conference Report, Oct. 1974, p. 30).

Elder James E. Faust, of the Quorum of the Twelve Apostles, has given us these insights regarding our ability to resist the tempter's power: "We all have an inner braking system that will stop us before we follow Satan too far down the wrong road. It is the still, small voice which is within us. But once we have succumbed, the braking system begins to leak brake fluid and our stopping mechanism becomes weak and ineffective." (*Ensign,* Nov. 1987, p. 34.)

An important aspect of obtaining and keeping the Spirit and of coming unto Christ is prayer. The Lord has told us that "the Spirit shall be given unto you by the prayer of faith" (D&C 42:14). Those who neglect their prayers remain in a "carnal and sinful state" (Mosiah 26:4).

Another way to draw near to our Father in Heaven and to "come unto Christ" is through regular reading and pondering of the scriptures. To get full value from the scriptures, we must search them. This will not come from occasionally using them as quote books or fillers for a talk. We are told to "feast upon the words of Christ; for behold, the words of Christ will tell you all things what ye should do" (2 Nephi 32:3).

Have you ever thought that when you search the scriptures you are hearing the voice of the Lord? Ponder these words from the Doctrine and Covenants:

> And I, Jesus Christ, your Lord and your God, have spoken it.
>
> These words are not of men nor of man, but of me. . . .
>
> For *it is my voice* which speaketh them unto you; for they are given by my Spirit unto you, and by my power you can read them one to another. . . .
>
> Wherefore, you can testify that *you have heard my voice,* and know my words. (D&C 18:33–36; italics added.)

Read the scriptures as if the Lord were speaking to you directly and you will "hear" His voice. If He is directing counsel to a specific person, replace that individual's name with yours and see how the counsel applies.

Keep in mind the Lord's admonition to "draw near unto me and I will draw near unto you; seek me diligently and ye shall find me; ask, and ye shall receive; knock, and it shall be opened unto you" (D&C 88:63).

Remember that perfection is a process. It is not an instantaneous product. Elder Dallin H. Oaks, of the

Quorum of the Twelve Apostles, has observed: "Spirituality is not acquired suddenly. It is the consequence of a succession of right choices. It is the harvest of a righteous life." (*Ensign*, Nov. 1985, p. 63.)

Another member of the Quorum of the Twelve Apostles, Elder Marvin J. Ashton, has taught us that "it is a fact of life that the direction in which we are moving is more important than where we are" (*Ensign*, May 1987, p. 67).

To "come unto Christ" is to continually seek to be like Him and not to be discouraged with the mistakes of mortality. I was impressed with the words of a newly called member of the Quorum of the Twelve Apostles some years ago. While speaking to a group of students, he said that some had asked him what it meant to be a "special witness of Jesus Christ." His response was, "It means I am *trying* to do my best to follow the Savior." Then he added, "And I emphasize the word *trying*!" This humble man did not proclaim perfection. He simply said he was striving to do what was right.

If you have occasional setbacks in sin, recognize that they need not be permanent! Once you have slipped in sin, you do not have to continue to slide. Elder Boyd K. Packer has said:

> It is contrary to the order of heaven for any soul to be locked into compulsive, immoral behavior with no way out!
>
> It *is* consistent with the workings of the adversary to deceive you into believing that you *are*. (*Ensign*, Nov. 1986, p. 18.)

Another of Lucifer's lies was commented on by Elder James E. Faust: "One of Satan's approaches is to persuade a person who has transgressed that there is no hope of forgiveness. But there is always hope. Most sins, no matter how grievous, may be repented of if the desire is sincere enough." (*Ensign,* Nov. 1987, p. 35.)

If you are burdened with sorrow, guilt, despair, unhappiness, or loneliness, "come unto Christ" and be relieved. For He has said:

> Come unto me, all ye that labour and are heavy laden, and I will give you rest.
>
> Take my yoke upon you, and learn of me; for I am meek and lowly in heart: and ye shall find rest unto your souls.
>
> For my yoke is easy, and my burden is light. (Matthew 11:28–30.)

Following Christ is the only way for you to fulfill your divine potential, both in this life and in the eternal worlds to come. *This is a time for youth who are committed to Christ.* President Ezra Taft Benson has observed: "We are meeting the adversary every day. The challenge of this era will rival any of the past, and these challenges will increase both spiritually and temporally. We must be close to Christ, we must daily take His name upon us, always remember Him, and keep His commandments." (*Ensign,* Nov. 1987, p. 85.)

To follow this counsel and "come unto Christ" is your only course of safety. It is also the only way to return to our Father (see John 14:6).

> And again I would exhort you that ye would *come unto Christ*, and lay hold upon every good gift, and touch not the evil gift, nor the unclean thing. . . .
>
> Yea, *come unto Christ*, and be perfected in him, and deny yourselves of all ungodliness; and if ye shall deny yourselves of all ungodliness, and love God with all your might, mind and strength, then is his grace sufficient for you, that by his grace ye may be perfect in Christ; and if by the grace of God ye are perfect in Christ, ye can in nowise deny the power of God. (Moroni 10:30, 32; italics added.)

Index

— W —

— Z —